Going
The Distance - No Parts
Left Behind

Your Epic Quest
How to Find Wholeness, Healing,
Purpose, and Abundance

FADHWA YUSUF

First printing, 2024.

Printed by The Gems Of life Inc. Canada

Kitchener, ON, Canada

https://www.thegemsoflife.com/

FOREWORD

Fadhwa Yusuf, the founder of Gems of Life Inc., emerged as a prominent figure among influencers and motivators. Her unique approach, deeply rooted in personal values and the power of the inner and higher self, has become a beacon of hope for many. Her work extends beyond her clients, reaching anyone seeking a transformative journey. She radiates life, love, and blessings as a celebrated torchbearer.

Fadhwa's journey radiates hope and success, inviting readers to accompany her on this profound journey. In these pages, she reveals the depths of her heart and guides us through the trials and triumphs of her life toward her higher, authentic self. She has chosen vulnerability, inviting readers to understand the depths of pain, struggle, and angst. By sharing her journey, she encourages us to embrace our vulnerability, allowing our higher selves to be the teacher, to guide and heal our wounded, unfulfilled selves.

She invites us into her world with remarkable vulnerability, where old wounds and long-held hurts have been confronted and transformed. Her story is a testament to the resilience of the human spirit and the power of embracing one's inner and higher self.

Fadhwa has painstakingly opened her heart, exposing old wounds, long-held hurts, and deep brokenness. Like a phoenix rising from the ashes, she has transformed her suffering into a path toward healing and wholeness. With unwavering optimism, she constantly anticipates a brighter day, a more fruitful future, and a glorious outcome. She extends an invitation to her readers to embrace a mindset of transformative positivity and resilient optimism, embodying the spirit of hope and faith.

This brilliant author presents to her readers the need for contemplative positioning, a willingness to be curious, and inner conversations that nurture personal growth, leading to a higher self and a more glorious outcome.

She urges her readers to dare to engage in an internal war between the past and the future and between the loss and a better and more fulfilling future. Her story is a testament to the power of personal growth, where the best version of oneself emerges from the ashes. Her words have the power to inspire us all to be more open to change and to embrace it willingly.

This author has courageously revealed the impact of her struggles. Through her vulnerability, she has led the way in her transformation, spreading its positive influence on her children, clients, friends, family and readers alike.

This positive, forward-tilting testimony of this talented young twenty-first-century leader in her generation has gifted her readers with a totally new concept of the workings of one's inner self. It is there that the most significant challenges are faced and overcome.

We follow such leaders, and together, we will succeed, thrive, and evolve into individuals whose inner resilience drives significant influence and meaningful change, transforming our lives and shaping a brighter world.

The world eagerly awaits "Going the Distance, No Parts Left Behind," led by visionary leaders like this gifted author.

Dr. Patricia Morgan

DEDICATION

With love and gratitude, I dedicate this book to my daughter Hodhan and son Hamza, my two beautiful children who remind me every day that I am still growing.

To my parents, thank you for the gift of life you have given and blessed me with.

And to you, congratulations on going the distance, and for believing in your highest version. Your Epic Quest already started the moment you picked up this book. Together, let's embark on our greatest life quest, an epic journey toward healing, wholeness, purpose and abundance, remember your higher version is non-negotiable.

Going
The Distance - No Parts
Left Behind

Your Epic Quest
How to Find Wholeness, Healing,
Purpose, and Abundance

FADHWA YUSUF

TABLE OF CONTENTS

INTRODUCTION

2017 was a year when I was caught in a storm of emotions: sadness, loneliness, and a deep sense of loss. I was living in a fog, unable to connect with those around me. I did not understand what was happening or how to go about fixing it. On one occasion, I stood at the window waiting for my daughter to return. When she stumbled and fell, I watched as she tearfully made her way back to the house. I didn't move; I just watched. I felt numb and detached from her pain. I didn't feel compelled to comfort her. At that moment, feelings of guilt and shame made me curious as to the cause of my indifference.

What was happening to me? Where did my protective instincts go? Why couldn't I feel anything?

The detachment and disconnection were alarming.

Somewhere along my journey, I had lost touch with myself.

That moment sparked my awakening. I realized I had been merely existing, going through each day without truly feeling or living. Despite being a dedicated mother and facing the challenges of single parenthood. I had lost sight of who I was. I was disconnected from myself and did not realize I was holding onto feelings and beliefs that shaped my life.

I found myself asking: Is this it? Is this what my life has come to?

I had to act quickly. I sold what I could, gave up the comfort of my home, and bought a one-way ticket to Africa with my two children. Everyone thought I had lost it. But can you lose what is already lost? I was on a self-rescue mission, desperate to hear my laughter again, to find myself and reconnect with who I truly am.

I took off. There was no plan B.

Three months later, in Africa, a pivotal moment reminded me of who I used to be. The video showed me laughing while watering the garden. The sound of happiness and joy was so familiar.

I wondered where that person had gone. I was buried under layers of disconnection. The revelation I sought was already within me, waiting to be rediscovered. The joy, happiness, and laughter were all still inside me. Realizing this was possible fueled my hunger for change and growth.

When I returned to Canada in 2019, I faced another uphill battle with homelessness, unemployment, and financial instability. But this time, I refused to let survival dictate my path. I embraced the challenge with a burning fire, knowing true fulfillment lay in embracing my highest self.

Fueled by newfound clarity, I began a journey of self-discovery, determined to break free from the chains of survival. I invested in my personal growth despite my uncertain circumstances. Survival was no longer an option; I was thirsty for knowledge and hungry for growth. I understood that my current knowledge wasn't enough to bring change; I needed new information. With each step forward, I found my strength and resilience. I was committed to going the distance and breaking free from survival.

Saying yes to my highest self, opened doors I never thought possible. It showed me the power of resilience and unwavering belief that we can rewrite our stories. As I stand here today, sharing my journey, I am living proof of the transformative power of embracing our true, highest selves.

There is no story you have told yourself that you can't change, no experience you have lived that you can't recreate. Your higher self is always ahead of you.

Embrace yourself; you are in for your biggest revelation. Your higher self is revealing itself to you even now. I accomplished things I never thought I could by saying yes to my highest self. This showed me that we can change our lives.

Today, as I share my story, I am proof that embracing who we truly are can transform our lives. Amid the struggles, there is a glimmer of faith—a realization that you have the power to change your story. It starts with saying YES to yourself! This book is about that—a guide to help you change the narrative of your story on your terms.

AUTHOR'S NOTE

What if you knew that the dreams you hold in your heart already exist? What if you knew the highest version of yourself is present right now? What if you knew, you were unstoppable, and nothing was holding you back from being your highest self? What if you knew this to be true in every part of your being?

Imagine bringing your deepest desires to life exactly as you always dreamed. By manifesting your soul's vision, you attract abundance into your life. You will find yourself filled with gratitude and joy when witnessing the incredible life you've created. You will be in awe, amazed at how your vision and desires have come true.

Imagine manifesting your vision exactly as you've always desired. The abundance flowing in your life includes the gift of time. Time is on your side, dancing with you, always showing up for you, asking, "What else do you want me to deliver?"

Time delivers your desires—every time.

You have the power to create anything you desire. Nothing is holding you back from making your vision come true. You know with certainty that time is on your side and your dreams, desires, and goals already exist.

Everything you want, including the version of yourself you aspire to be, already exists. The version of you that wants wealth is already here. The version of you that wants to connect with your soulmate is already here. The version of you that wants to contribute is here. These versions of you already exist. What if you knew that the version of yourself that is successful in both your personal and professional life is already here?

What if you knew for sure that you are abundantly wealthy in all areas of your life? If you knew this for certain, how would your life be different today?

How would you show up today? How would you show up differently? What would you do differently today? How would you be your highest self today?

What would you want to create, knowing nothing is stopping you from achieving your desires? Think about any limiting beliefs you have about yourself, and imagine they no longer exist. How would your life be different?

If you believe time is on your side, what would you like time to deliver to you? How would you use time to create your desires? If you knew time could deliver anything, what would you ask for?

Knowing that time will deliver what you spend time on, what would you focus on? Knowing that everything you envision, and desire already exists, what do you want to create? If you knew that everything existed, what would you have done differently? What new beliefs would you develop?

How would your highest self, show up differently? And how would you support your highest self? I trust you are now curious about the abundance of possibilities.

I will share the steps you need to take to create the life you desire and manifest exactly what you want. Approach this with curiosity and openness.

It only takes a moment to transform your life, to change its direction. Notice where your life is heading right now. Focus on any area you want to transform, and you will begin to see changes in how you show up.

You will start taking action without limitations and working with time instead of managing or squeezing it. You will find yourself in alignment with time and in a good relationship with it. Why the shift and change in direction?

Here's why.

You will build relationships and connect with your highest self. This higher self understands the importance of time. Remember, time will deliver what you spend time on.

I recognize when it's time for my current self to step aside so my highest self can take over. My current self hasn't reached its fullest potential yet. To tap into my highest potential, my current self must step aside and let my higher self take over.

I understand I can't fully achieve my epic vision at the speed I want. To realize my vision, it's crucial to work with time so it can deliver my vision faster. For this to happen, my highest self must work in harmony with time.

Recognize that time works with you. Time is generous, and we'll talk more about this in later chapters. For now, trust that time is here to work with you and deliver what you spend time on.

You can work with time and develop a healthy relationship with it instead of squeezing and managing it. No matter what you do, time stays the same. It never misses a beat. Time keeps moving, never stops, and always shows up.

Now imagine this higher version that flows within you, full of creativity, ideas, and inspiration. Imagine this higher version of you has the freedom and flexibility to live a life of your design. As abundance flows into your life, you marvel at how quickly it keeps coming.

As you observe your life, are you leading a fulfilling life? Have you discovered your purpose? Have you found inspiration in everything you do?

CHAPTER ONE
The Highest Version of Yourself

Connecting to your highest version is non-negotiable.

Ibelieve there is always a higher version of yourself ready to step in. Are you willing to step aside and let that happen?

Your current version has peaked; it's time for your next version to step in and replace it. Being your highest self is key to creating the vision your soul desires. Your highest version already exists, and it's important to create your vision from there.

Don't base your vision on your current circumstances. Like a fish in a pond, your vision may be limited by your current understanding. How can you expect change if you keep working with the same information? To create something truly extraordinary, you need to seek out the full spectrum of possibilities beyond your current view.

You must learn to recognize when a version of yourself has reached its limit and can't progress further. Create space for the highest version to step in. Understand when you've reached a point where you can't go further. At that moment, step aside and let the next version of yourself take over and continue your journey. Recognize when your highest version is ready to take over and push you even further.

At every stage of life, there is a version of yourself that holds the essential knowledge you need to grow and achieve your goals. However, this version is only accessible at certain points in your life. You must recognize when you reach these points and be open to embracing the higher version of yourself that is ready to step in.

This higher version holds the key to the knowledge you need to achieve your desired outcomes. Remember, your higher version has access to information and insights you haven't accessed yet.

When you keep that door closed, you block yourself from the opportunity to grow and change your life. But when you open the door and welcome your highest version, allowing your current version to step aside, you give yourself a chance for new growth and opportunities.

By doing so, you tell your highest version: I am ready to receive you.

I am ready to learn. I am not competing with you; we are working together, not against each other. I am your student, and you are my guide. Together, we can achieve our vision.

I first realized a part of me was searching for meaning and purpose in 2017. There was a version of me that knew what I didn't. This version had already gone the distance. I had to let my current self step aside for that version to show up.

Previous versions of myself had achieved great things, but for the higher version to emerge, I had to learn when to let go of my current self. I went through this process in 2017, but I didn't have the awareness and understanding that I do now.

I took that step forward to let my highest self emerge. It's a process of letting go of past versions and allowing new ones to come forward.

Your higher self communicates with you. The question is, are you listening when it says:

> "I'm getting you out of here. You've been stuck in this space for too long. I'm pulling you out of this situation or mess."

Are you listening when it says:

> "Let me in. I know the path. I have gone the distance."

Do you recognize when your higher self speaks to you?

Often, you resist and ignore the call until it becomes a rescue mission. That's what happened to me—I was in a place where I didn't know what was pulling me, yet the call was loud and clear:

> "Step aside; it's time to step out and step up. You need to step outside of this space. There's no room here for you to step up. You must step out and create the space you need to step up."

My higher self saved me. Back in 2017, I felt sad, empty, lost, and lonely. It was all too much, completely unfamiliar territory for me.

But it sparked my curiosity:

What is happening to me? Who am I? When did I lose myself?

Unaware that I was reaching out to my higher self, somehow, my call was answered. I summoned, and my higher self listened and responded. Remember, your higher self has been through it all, understands what you may not, and has access to knowledge you haven't acquired yet.

My higher self came to me, encouraging me to step forward so it could step in:

*"I'm going to lift you out of this situation, and someday you'll
understand why."*

As you start making moves towards progress, others might think
you're acting strangely for doing what needs to be done. Stepping
out means leaving behind the comfort of familiarity while stepping
up demands facing discomfort and taking challenging actions.

For me, this meant leaving everything behind and buying a one-
way ticket to Africa for myself and my children. After all, my higher
self had already paved the way and knew where we were headed. I'll
delve deeper into this in the upcoming chapters.

For now, remember it's crucial to make room for your higher self
to step in while allowing your current self to step out.

Before returning to Canada, I had spent eighteen months in
Africa. The first three months were about rejuvenating my health;
all I did was eat, sleep, and soak in the sun. Three months later, I
felt energized enough to find work. I was in a city I knew nothing of
and had no friends to talk to; I was fortunate enough to stay with my
parents, who had left the UK for the holidays and come to Africa.
It was special, especially with my children. It was the longest we had
spent with my parents and staying close to them brought comfort to
my heart. There was a level of relief from day-to-day stress. I didn't
have to worry about a lot of things; I had the support I needed at the
time to find myself and rediscover my purpose.

During my time in Africa, I experienced a significant shift in
perspective. I had no social connections; I lived in a place where
it's not what but who you know that matters. Three months later,
I found a job as the operations manager of a five-star hotel. The
work culture was challenging, so I left and founded my consulting
firm three months later. I made great connections, even standing

with the president during the ribbon cutting. 'How did I accomplish this quickly?' I asked myself. What prevented me from such accomplishments in Canada? I was alive with a sense of purpose. I was making a difference. I was building relationships. I was in charge of my life; where did these versions disappear to in Canada? This journey not only led to professional growth but also a deeper understanding of myself and my capabilities.

When I returned from Africa in 2019, I had no home, no job, and no money, so I temporarily stayed at my family's place. I distinctly remember telling myself:

This isn't the end for me. I refuse to return to who I used to be—I'm determined to keep pushing forward in life.

I realized my current knowledge wasn't enough to change my life's direction. My understanding was limited, and I lacked what I needed to reach my goals. I felt like a fish in a pond, stuck within its boundaries, unable to swim beyond. Little did I know, while I was reaching out to my highest self, it was also speaking to me, saying:

> "You've come a long way with what you know. I've been through it all and know the path ahead. It's time to step out of your comfort zone and rise to the challenge. Let me help you."

Creating the space for this to happen is crucial. I was eager for something new. I wanted to create different outcomes and results in my life. The idea of going back to 2017 scared me. I knew if I didn't step aside and let my higher self guide me, I would lose myself again. That was no longer an option. I noticed that between 2017 and 2019, I had changed. There was a spark inside me, and I wasn't about to dim it. It was the first time I felt truly alive. I wanted more.

Even though I wasn't sure what it looked like, I knew there was more to life than what I had imagined for myself.

I realized it was time to let my next version step in. To grow and move to the next level, you must create space for your higher self to guide you.

You might not have enough information to take your life to the next level, but a version of you has already achieved your goals. This version will guide you and show you the steps to create the life you want. You'll know it's working when everything starts falling into place.

Your highest self will help you gain the knowledge, wisdom, and information needed to achieve your goals. As you progress, you'll notice a shift and growth within you, and your vision for your life will start to come true in ways you never imagined.

Since then, my highest self has led me on a journey of self-discovery, learning, growth, healing, and wisdom. Most importantly, it has taught me the importance of self-acceptance.

Have you ever felt like you hit an invisible wall in your life? Did you know when to step aside and let your highest self take over?

It's crucial to understand that you are the highest version of yourself today compared to yesterday. But to keep growing and improving, you must listen to that inner voice urging you to be the best version of yourself. If you ignore your highest self, you'll eventually hit an invisible wall and struggle to move forward.

When you are in pain, suffering, and struggling in life, it means you've ignored your highest calling. You've closed the doors for your best self to step in. It means you are not willing to listen and step aside.

I invite you to recognize where you are today. Your current self is the result of your journey so far. Every step you've taken and every decision you've made has brought you to this point. Even if you didn't realize it then, each step and choice caused a shift in your life.

So, embrace your highest version, the one that has gone the distance with you.

Now, think back to that moment, what did you do differently?

Chances are you reached a point where you said: ENOUGH.

I have come this far; change must happen for me to get the results I want.

A shift happened without you realizing it. It was your highest self-stepping in and saying: "Thank you for the invitation. I heard you, and I'm here. I have come a long way, and you'll be amazed at what you're about to discover."

Remember, where you are now is yesterday's highest version. Your highest self has already gone through what you're experiencing now. The mistake is relying on yesterday's highest version to carry you through today and into the future. You need to aim for tomorrow's highest version of yourself to achieve true fulfillment and reach your goals. This version of you has experienced things you haven't yet and has gone the distance.

Even if you don't have all the answers or solutions to life's challenges, your highest self has overcome these challenges, knows what's possible for you, gained wisdom, and achieved the outcomes you want. When you're stuck with unhelpful beliefs and thoughts, don't worry about things you can't control. Instead, listen to the inner voice calling you, which says: *If only you'd let me in.*

Opportunities are waiting for you on the other side of the wall. Connecting to your highest version is key to manifesting your vision. It's essential. Remember, you cannot rely on your past and current selves to create your epic vision—they are limited and don't have the resources you need. You need to connect to your highest version, the one that has gone the distance and manifested your vision.

It's important to connect to your highest version if you want to change your results and create different outcomes in your life. You need your highest version to create your vision.

Your highest version is the one that creates your vision.

So, what does that mean for you?

Knowing with certainty that your highest version already exists is essential, and creating an epic vision from that version is crucial. You don't create your vision from where you are now. You are like a fish in a pond, seeing with a limited lens, and your vision is limited.

It's important to connect with your highest version to manifest your vision. You must embody your highest self. You need to show up as your highest self to create the vision your soul desires. There is a higher version of you at every point in your life. Do you recognize when your higher self-shows up? It's being certain that your highest self has manifested the life you desire. When your highest self-knocks on your door, are you listening?

When it calls out to you and says: *I got you... open the door and let me in. I've been where you are. I've been where you're heading. I know everything you need to know. What if I show you a faster way to get what you want? I've manifested your desires.*

At every stage of your life, there is a higher version of you that has gone the distance, gained experience, grown, evolved, and transformed.

Looking back on my life, I realize I have gone through many versions of myself and am amazed. When I look back at who I was in 2017, I never imagined that the person I would become already existed within me. It took the 2024 version of me to realize how much I have grown and changed. In 2017, I couldn't have imagined the person I would become in 2024, but now I see that version of myself already existed.

This realization made me reflect on the past version of myself. Until that moment, my past selves wanted to change my future, but I now see that it wasn't possible. I used to do things the same way and expect different outcomes. To break the cycle, I learned my current self needed to step aside and let the next version take over.

The first time I felt a deep sense of loneliness and loss was in 2017; I couldn't explain the void inside. However, I also realized I needed to reset my life. Experiencing the loss of self-helped me reset. It was a moment of self-liberation, self- rescue, and bold choices; it was when I uttered these words: This is not my ending.

I wanted to rediscover myself and find my true passions. Without realizing it, a more evolved version of me heard my calling at that moment and stepped in. I stepped back, letting this new version, which had already overcome many challenges, take over. I was unaware of the surprising discovery that awaited me about my true passions and strengths, a path that would set me on a path of self-discovery, helping me grow and evolve even further.

Your highest version can take you further and reveal what is possible. It can pull you out of darkness and drive you to take the next step. I encourage you to explore your current self. Where do you stand right now? What thoughts or feelings come up as you read this? Ask yourself if you rely on past versions to move forward.

Remember that your current knowledge, wisdom, and experiences have brought you to where you are today, but they might not be enough to propel you forward. A higher version of yourself exists and is always available to you. Your highest self evolves with you. Reflect on this: the version of yourself today was shaped by your past.

Take a moment to explore and recognize the immense potential within you. You have a higher version of yourself that has already overcome challenges, gained knowledge and wisdom, and has manifested the life your soul desires. Embrace the certainty that this higher version has already achieved your goals and aspirations. Believe that you can move toward making your dreams a reality.

How would you see yourself if you were certain that a higher version of you already existed? This knowledge has the power to completely shift your self-perception.

Even at my lowest point, when I didn't know what to do or where to turn, I reminded myself this was not the end of my story.

Deep inside, I know my higher self exists and is ready to take control. I find comfort and assurance in knowing that my highest version is already within me. I must connect with this higher self to manifest my soul's desires and reach my full potential. This is non-negotiable.

I invite you to make space for your higher self to step in. Step aside, watch, observe, and learn. Be curious, say yes to yourself, and let your elevated self lift you up. Remember, there's no need to hold onto a version of yourself that you've outgrown.

Like the sun behind clouds, your brilliance is hidden, and your potential obscured, unable to shine fully to reveal the warmth and light within you. But your highest version is like the sun breaking through the clouds—free and liberated. It can be whatever it chooses to be. The possibilities are limitless.

An interesting story I want to share:

On New Year's Day, I decided to record a message wishing everyone a happy New Year. I recorded the first two videos but deleted both because I wasn't sure if my message was coming across how I wanted it to. Before recording a third video, I paused to reflect on what was missing. Then, it hit me.

I realized that the version of myself in the recording was the one that had stepped aside, still trying to drive the conversation.

Meanwhile, my higher self, who wanted to deliver the message, struggled to step in.

You can fully show up as the highest version of yourself at any given moment.

The dilemma was that the version speaking was a past version, while the version that wanted to speak was my highest self—the one that has manifested my vision gained wisdom and gone the distance. This highest version struggled to show up because the past version wouldn't step aside.

Eventually, the past version noticed its struggle and realized it was trying to be something it hadn't yet evolved into. Once the past version understood this, it finally stepped aside. Only then could the current version say:

> *I'm trying to be you when I'm not. I'm stepping aside, and I appreciate that you're not taking over me; you are an expansion of me.*

There is a conflict between two versions of yourself. One has made significant progress but now feels dismissed as it's expected to step aside. The highest version wants to step in and propel you forward, but the past versions won't give up without resistance.

It's important to recognize when this resistance occurs. If you don't, your highest version can't step in, and your struggles will continue. Some of us struggle to move on or embrace change. We hold on to what we're familiar with, resisting the unknown and limiting ourselves from new possibilities. We are like fish in a pond, unable to explore beyond our limited surroundings.

The version of you that needs to step aside must understand they are not being rejected or dismissed. Instead, you are saying to your past version, *You are an expansion of me.* Each version is an expansion of you.

The current version is an expanded part of your highest version, continually growing and evolving. The joy in this process is when the current version says to the higher version, *I appreciate you without feeling dismissed, and I am honoured to be on this journey with you. I get to witness your growth and expansion.*

It's beautiful to witness the connection between the two versions, working together and sharing information without conflict. It's affirming:

As a witness, I am not just an observer but a part of this journey. Now, I have the privilege to see the legacy you are creating, a legacy we all share.

Each version creates and carries a legacy, with your highest version continuing to develop it. This powerful realization allows the higher version to step in. Your story is never finished. Your life is always evolving, and you are constantly creating and rewriting your story: a new page, a new chapter.

Isn't it wonderful to recognize that your experiences shape your higher version? You are a co- creator in every chapter of your life. Every version of yourself has contributed to endless chapters. It's important to recognize and appreciate each version, as they've co-created and co-authored your life story and legacy, leading to who you are today.

Each version co-created the next. Each version co-authored the next chapter. Each version has a chapter; appreciate each version and the parts they contributed to your story. Each part is co-written with your highest version. Your story changes, shifts, and transforms with every chapter, shaping who you are today.

Returning to the recording:

I recognized the battle between the two versions as I recorded and deleted the videos. It was also beautiful to witness their dance, a precious moment when I stopped recording and paid attention to what was happening.

At that moment, the higher version acknowledged this and said:

> "Thank you for calling out to me. I appreciate you. Thank you for trusting me and making room for me to step in. Thank you for allowing me to be part of this journey with you and for inspiring me to be who I am today."

> "I wouldn't be here without you."

The higher version is now acknowledging past versions and finally says:

> "You created me. I am your legacy. You brought me here. I am a culmination of each of you. I represent each one of you. It is my honour, and I thank you for trusting me to step in and rewrite our story."

It was the moment the highest version said:

> "You're coming along. You are part of the legacy."

As soon as I hit record and started speaking, the message came through naturally and flawlessly. That was January 1st, 2024. The message was ten minutes long and consisted of information about creating the highest version of myself, sharing my experiences while recording, and the wisdom I gained.

The question now is, where do you begin? Remember, everything is connected. Each chapter connects to the highest version of yourself. There are chapters dedicated to parts that go into detail. To find wholeness again, you need to work with the parts so they can become whole and take on their original version. This way, you can become who you truly are—not just your authentic self, but your highest version.

Transformation happens when the limited or trapped parts change their beliefs and no longer occupy the space. An abundance of space is created when there is an expansive opening, ready to receive the abundance of your vision. This is the space you need for your highest version.

If you know your highest version exists, then you also know your vision has manifested. Everything is connected. Each chapter captures the design of your desired life and the manifestation of your epic vision.

You need to ask yourself, "Who do I need to be?" rather than "What do I need to do?" It's about knowing and working as a unified, wholesome embodiment of being.

Moment of Reflection

CHAPTER TWO
Introducing The Parts

Understand your parts. Stop trying to eliminate them; they are not your enemy.

When I talk about parts, I mean beliefs. Beliefs hold different narratives in your life, each playing a role. Some of the beliefs you hold represent stories that have shaped your life.

You gain more by doing this:

When the limiting part transforms into its original form, you gain an ally to help you manifest your vision and find inner peace and expansion, creating space for the abundance flowing into your life. You need this space; through this process, you gain much more than you started with.

Each part holds a story that has significantly impacted your life—a story you can reflect on and appreciate for its role in shaping your journey. These parts have defined how you live today. They have played crucial roles and made decisions that have shaped your life and made you who you are.

Each part has a role and a story. These parts witness your experiences of hurt, pain, and disappointment. Beneath these layers, they are resilient and courageous. They show up in every moment of your life.

When you engage in healing and self-discovery, invite all parts of yourself along. Remember, none should be left behind; each part plays a role in manifesting your desires. All versions of yourself must go the distance for true healing and self-discovery. So, take the time to acknowledge and work with each part for a complete and fulfilling journey.

No parts left behind means more than just recognizing what these parts are, their purpose, and their contribution to your life. There are no wrong parts; they all contribute to your life. These parts come in the form of beliefs, perceptions, and emotions like fear. They affect how you respond to situations and influence your emotions, actions, and outcomes in life.

To create a clear and epic vision of your life, it is essential to examine your life experiences, identify the roles these parts have played, and understand how they have influenced your daily experiences. This will help you move forward toward manifesting your vision.

Look at your life with curiosity and consider all aspects as keys to creating the outcomes you desire.

I've come to recognize that despite all my work, I focused a lot on eliminating and overcoming these parts. I've done a lot of healing, which has led me to greater self-understanding and self-discovery.

By exploring and understanding different parts, I realized they influenced my decisions, choices, and the people I was attracted to.

Communicate with the Parts

These parts influenced the outcomes and results I kept getting and attracting into my life. They affected my relationships, parenting, and overall quality of life. I felt lost, without purpose, and barely existing.

Little did I know that the results and outcomes in my life were in complete alignment with these unknown parts. I was unaware of them, unable to recognize their messages.

I was not in tune with the way these parts communicated, as I lacked understanding and hadn't developed the language they spoke. I didn't know how to use such a language to communicate with them.

Learning how to communicate with different parts is crucial. Bringing all these parts with you on your journey without leaving any behind is essential. To connect and understand these parts you must develop a language with them.

By doing so, you can establish a healthy and harmonious relationship with these parts. Communicating with all aspects of your being is an art you must master. The key to manifesting your vision is to ensure that every part is on board, and none are left behind.

I've learned that temporary solutions act like bandages when eliminating these parts. You will continue to hold onto limiting beliefs if you attempt to eliminate the parts that hold those beliefs. Unless you learn to communicate with these parts, eliminating them is just a temporary fix.

Eliminating the Parts

The more you try to uproot, eliminate, and get rid of these parts, the farther you move from your intended goal and vision. You've learned to communicate with these parts through aggression, suppression, and elimination. This method won't work in the long run. It might provide a temporary fix, but you'll keep getting the same or worse results.

You might wonder why things aren't going your way despite spending all your energy, attention, focus, and money on eliminating these parts. Take time to develop a language to communicate with them. Only then will your life path start to take a different direction. Think about it: you want to get rid of the part that brought you here.

By the time you finish reading this book, you'll develop a healthy relationship with these different parts, and your entire life will transform. All I ask is that you keep an open mind. If you feel some resistance, that's a part communicating with you. This is an excellent opportunity to develop a language to communicate with that resistant part.

The Gatekeepers

These gatekeepers communicate with each other and protect the parts from any perceived threat. What happens is that the gatekeeper takes over to shield the part from harm.

It's important to understand that just arming yourself with knowledge and trying to eradicate these parts without understanding their purpose and function can be counterproductive. Instead, we must approach these parts with compassion and a willingness to work with them.

Eliminating these parts is not the only way to overcome limiting beliefs, doubts, or fears. Anytime there's a threat to any part, the gatekeeper will step up and protect it. Trying to uproot these parts causes more harm than good, creating a further disconnect with them.

Remember, there is no such thing as overcoming a limiting belief, eliminating a belief around fear, getting rid of fear, or overcoming the belief around abandonment. This way of communicating with these parts will not get you the results you want and desire.

By eliminating these parts from your life you are saying, I have a vision in life, and to achieve it, I must eliminate you. You are slowing me down, holding me back, and limiting me. By doing this, you are telling these parts that they have no place in your journey and are no longer needed. Can you relate to that?

I can. I spent time and money trying to eliminate these parts from my life. I had dreams and felt these parts were limiting my ability to manifest my vision. However, I found myself further away from achieving it. By doing this, you are harming these parts and continue to attract negative consequences in your life's outcomes.

Diving deeper into your parts. What's their story?

You want to recognize these parts because they have a role to play. They bring value and meaning to your life. However, they may not be serving your best interests or helping you achieve your goals.

You cannot ignore that these parts played a massive role in your life when you were younger. There was a time when these parts were of great value, and they are still doing what they know best. These parts don't realize that you have grown into a capable adult who can care for yourself. That's why they keep coming back to rescue you whenever you are in a difficult situation.

You co-wrote the story with the parts, and the parts co-wrote your story.

You need to understand their story. These parts have a compelling story you are part of—you co-wrote and are living it.

You're making a serious mistake if you think you can rewrite your story without these parts. These parts have power. They have been your co-pilots, co-drivers, and co-writers in life. They have a massive stake in this; you can't just say they are of no value, no longer needed, and can be eliminated.

What will happen then? All the parts you didn't know about will show up. These parts have the power to hold you back.

Ever wonder why you sometimes feel stuck? You might ask yourself, "Why?" and second-guess your work and commitment, thinking, "I got rid of fear and limiting beliefs, yet I'm still trapped."

Did you think you wrote your life story on your own? Did you think you could rewrite it without these parts? Is it possible to rewrite your story without including these parts and giving them credit?

Be curious about these parts. Get to know them better. Notice which parts are more present in your life: the silent gatekeepers, the ones filled with rage, the disconnected parts, and the limiting parts that show up today.

How?

Start journaling and take note of these parts. You need to know them to communicate with them in a way that transforms you both.

Remember, going the distance means leaving no parts behind and knowing you can manifest anything you desire without limitations.

Now, let's get to know these parts and how they show up in your life. Each part layer has a story that you are a part of. Approach these parts like you would a baby or a child—with curiosity, openness, compassion, and a willingness to learn and explore. Notice what shows up, as each part has its own layers.

These parts hold the key to accessing the highest version of yourself and manifesting your vision.

Reflective questions reconcile with the parts.

You can't rewrite your story or go the distance without reconciling and re-engaging with these parts. How do you reconcile with these parts? How do you rewrite and co-author your story? How do you manifest your vision and become the best version of yourself without eliminating any parts?

Working with the Parts

I was committed to healing my wounds, working on myself, and doing the inner work. However, I was unaware of the deep, unresolved wounds that my triggered parts held on to and didn't know how to resolve them. Despite my constant struggle, I stayed committed to understanding the unresolved emotional wounds linked to my inner child's experiences.

I had developed a level of consciousness and awareness, able to detect when I was triggered. I used different healing methods to address the triggered parts, but I still found myself highly activated repeatedly, and the wounds remained unresolved.

Something was missing. My inner child's wounded parts were still attached to the past and had not yet healed. I realized I couldn't give these parts the care and attention they desperately needed. They needed healing, and I needed to find a way to provide it. Despite using numerous healing methods, I still faced the same or similar wounds. But I was willing to put in the work. I was committed to healing, developing a relationship with my inner child, connecting with different parts of myself, and gaining a deeper understanding of the stories I told myself.

I kept wondering: How do I overcome this?

How can I heal the wounded parts? What do I need to do to prevent the triggered parts from reactivating and resurfacing?

The inner child's experiences hold the wounded parts, the beliefs, or emotions that are constantly triggered. Like many others, I was still figuring it out, grappling with my own challenges. For instance, I struggled with self-doubt and fear of the unknown. It's a journey many of us share—a journey that can often feel isolating, but we're not alone in this struggle.

During this journey, I have met individuals who are brilliant, capable, and competent. They possess immense potential, yet they, too, face their own battles. In my interactions with different people, I often encounter thought- provoking questions: "Why are you limiting yourself and not fully using your potential? Why are you playing small?" My response would be, "I don't know what's stopping me." Deep down, I know I'm capable and have what it takes, but I can't seem to get past the invisible wall. I was reminded that I have what it takes to succeed, thrive, and manifest my vision.

Fish in a Pond

Here we are in our reality, like fish in a pond, content in our confined space. We might think we're doing great, but this pond is just an analogy. It's all we know, and we've grown so used to it that we don't see the abundance of possibilities available.

Like fish in a pond, we're unaware of the limitations of our confined space. But what if we could see beyond? What if we realized the abundance of possibilities available to us?

We are drawn to familiarity, comfort, safety, and security. But this 'comfort zone' can be more limiting than we realize. Just as the pond is meant to be temporary, we've settled into a space that's comfortable but also holds us back from tapping into the vast possibilities.

These parts' functions were meant to be temporary.

They are like fish in a pond; that's all they know because they haven't experienced the abundance available. These parts only understand what is familiar to them. They seek safety and comfort. When you disrupt this comfort and safety, these parts see it as a threat.

Bringing these parts to your vision is like taking a fish out of a pond and showing it the ocean. What are the chances the fish will return to the confinement of the pond? When you show the fish the abundance of the ocean, it will jump into the sea with excitement.

That's the approach you want for these parts—to empower them and create a different vision.

Moment of Reflection

CHAPTER THREE
The Belief and Emotional Parts

Your conditioning shapes the way you act, think, and feel.

Have you ever wondered what beliefs might be holding you back from becoming the best version of yourself? Can you identify the beliefs that act as barriers preventing you from achieving your life goals, objectives, and desires? These are the 'limiting beliefs' we need to overcome. For example, a common limiting belief could be, "I'm not smart enough to succeed in my career." Can you think of any beliefs that are holding you back?

When I talk about parts, I'm talking about beliefs. The beliefs you hold are often unconscious, meaning you're not fully aware of them. When you develop a higher level of consciousness, you become more aware of the conscious beliefs you hold, which are the ones you can actively work on changing.

Notice what I said—it was with great intention. I chose my words carefully. At times, we may think our beliefs are accurate and true.

Which is true for you? Notice the difference in language.

> You believe **the** beliefs you hold are accurate and true.
> VS
> You believe **your** beliefs are accurate and true.

Limiting beliefs are not yours to own; however, the moment you interpret a belief as yours, it becomes true for you—that's the moment you own it.

Beliefs are parts of your past experiences that may surface as limiting beliefs. These parts hold beliefs that come with a story, like:

> I am not good enough. I am not smart enough. I am unloved.
> I am not worthy enough. I am undeserving. I am insignificant.
> I am unseen or invisible. I am not valued.

Do any of these belief parts sound familiar to you?

These are just some examples of the beliefs you may be holding. They might manifest in your life and create results and outcomes you do not desire.

When an emotion is triggered, we often develop beliefs as a coping mechanism. These beliefs act as gatekeepers, rescuing us from the pain of the triggering emotion. It's a common response to believe 'I am not good enough' rather than face the pain.

It's not the event or circumstances that define us; our interpretation of the event and the meaning we assign to it triggers our emotions and beliefs. Our perception is the key.

For instance, if we interpret a failure as a sign of incompetence, it can trigger feelings of shame and reinforce the belief of inadequacy that we are not good enough.

When we are triggered, our familiar beliefs come to the rescue, making it seem safer to believe 'I am not good enough' than to face the pain of the triggering emotion. Beliefs are our comfort zone, while emotions are often unfamiliar territory.

We have not been taught to attune to our feelings but are very familiar with our beliefs. Most of us know these beliefs, but no one comfortably speaks of their emotions: I am sad, lonely, angry, or ashamed. However, we can achieve a more balanced emotional well-being by attuning to our feelings.

Understanding the many layers of the parts that hold your beliefs is crucial. Each belief has a unique story, and each part has a gatekeeper that ensures all parts are safe and not threatened. Trying to eradicate a limiting belief isn't a solution; it's barely scratching the surface.

The layers of beliefs show up in your body and mind as emotions, sensations, and thoughts. These parts are trapped and suppressed, leading to fear, anger, rage, sadness, guilt, and shame, as well as thoughts of not being good enough or unloved. It's common to encounter these emotions and beliefs at different points in life.

These are just some examples of trapped emotions that show up. These parts also influence behaviours like being a people pleaser, a fixer, or a perfectionist. Some parts feel compelled to shut down, disconnect, and detach.

Take a moment to notice the beliefs you are aware of and journal them. What are some conscious beliefs present in your life? Name the parts that hold these emotions.

These parts play a significant role in your life. While you may be aware of some, many remain in the shadows of your unconsciousness. These unconscious parts are the true drivers of your life outcomes. Contrary to what you might believe, it's not the conscious parts holding you back but the unconscious ones that limit your ability to achieve your vision and goals.

Sometimes, you find yourself trapped in a story. These stories and limiting beliefs can severely limit your potential for growth. Can you imagine the impact all these "parts"—the different aspects of your personality and emotions—have on your life?

I invite you to notice what happens when you experience fear, anger, sadness, shame, guilt, or any limiting belief. Take a moment to actively observe what happens to you when an emotion or limiting belief part is activated. If an emotion is present, what do you automatically resort to? What is your go-to response?

When you find yourself in a reactive state, where your emotions control your actions, it means you've entered an activated state. At this moment, the gatekeeper parts take over, and you lose the ability to be fully present and listen to what these activated parts are communicating to you. Without heightened awareness of the activated parts, you may not even recognize the triggers. This self-awareness is critical to understanding these parts.

Consider this: when the gatekeeper notices that the fear part is not acknowledged, it intervenes and brings in an overlooked part. This part then reacts by either suppressing or intensifying the fear, as it always does. Each part has a layer connected to another part, and each has a story. When you find yourself activated, it's a part of a part sending you a message. The goal is to develop relationships with these parts, not ignore them.

What happens when you silence or ignore a part? The more you avoid it, the more you'll suffer. Therefore, you must improve and develop your relationships with these parts. What is the meaning and purpose of the gatekeeper? The gatekeeper is a metaphorical term used in psychological self-help to describe a part of our psyche that acts as a protector.

The gatekeeper knows when to step in. Whenever there's a perceived threat to safety, the gatekeepers shield the parts with limiting beliefs or painful emotions. The gatekeeper, a protector of your emotional well-being, also serves to keep all parts safe, including yourself. As long as the gatekeeper's function is safety, the parts will not be free from their past but will continue to relive it. The gatekeepers believe their role is to provide a sense of safety, which is crucial. We must recognize that the gatekeepers are confined by limited beliefs and must be the first to be freed from limitations.

If you haven't developed a relationship with a part or a way to communicate with fear, for instance, you miss the opportunity to understand and address the needs and desires of these parts.

How does that happen?

Understand that we may hold onto stories we consider accurate, which are trapped parts that hold a belief that created the story. This understanding alone will allow you to recognize when a part of a belief resurfaces and activates your emotions and beliefs. This awareness is crucial to our growth.

Consider this: if a part's story revolves around beliefs of not being good enough, unworthy, unloved, or unwanted, the associated emotions will surface. You might experience guilt or shame linked to another part that holds blame around these emotions. This belief acts as a shield, masking the underlying pain with a narrative, and the gatekeepers will shield the part suppressing the pain associated with the emotion and belief.

The gatekeeper parts play a significant role in shifting attention from fear to self-blame. This self- blame often manifests as a belief that 'it must be my fault '. This belief is persistent because it convinces you that you've done something wrong, and the other person was right. Consequently, you may feel compelled to fix things and please others, which is also a part linked to another part. The compulsion to fix, please, even perfectionism, self-blame, and guilt, are also linked to another part.

Sometimes, instead of looking within, we shift blame to others. This is a defence mechanism.; a gatekeeper's role is to redirect attention away from your vulnerabilities. It's much easier to look outward rather than inward because it feels safer. The gatekeeper part's primary function is to protect you. These defence mechanisms are the gatekeepers' work; they are not enemies but protectors of the parts, tirelessly working to keep them safe from emotional harm. They are there to protect, not to judge.

The part that directs attention outward does so with a purpose: to shield another part from feeling pain. Consider what could happen if you confront fear parts head-on and try to uproot them completely. Can you imagine the outcome? You will unleash emotions and beliefs beyond your control, potentially overwhelming you. When that happens, the gatekeepers will come to the rescue, complicating your ability to manage activated emotions and beliefs.

Are you open to exploring or even questioning your current beliefs? Let's be clear: you can never get rid of fear. You may think you can and attempt to do so, but not in the way you have been taught.

But here's the empowering truth: shifting fear and limiting beliefs is possible, not by eliminating them but by changing their narrative on your life. When we talk about shifting fear or limiting beliefs, we must understand that no parts are left behind. This includes the parts that hold the beliefs and emotions.

They are all acknowledged and validated, but their influence on your actions and decisions can be altered. Going the distance is the journey toward manifesting your soul's desires, living your desired life, and creating outcomes aligned with purpose and meaning.

It means setting clear goals, taking consistent action, and staying committed despite challenges. It's about not giving up and pushing through until you achieve what you truly desire.

What if there is another way? Are you willing to explore other possibilities? Consider the potential for growth and new perspectives. Are you open to embracing the shift, even if it means questioning your current beliefs?

You are trying to go the distance with no parts on board. You have a vision, a dream, yet you're not manifesting your goals. You wonder why?

The process of going the distance with no parts left behind is not just about attaining your dreams. It's about embracing the challenges, setbacks, growth, and transformation along the way. You have a dream, a vision that you aspire to manifest. Yet, in your pursuit, you may find yourself focusing on eliminating what you perceive as limitations. However, it's important to remember that these perceived limitations are not holding you back but rather protecting you from harm and keeping you safe.

Each setback and challenge is influenced by a part whose role is to keep you safe, not limit you. Remember, you are not limited. Like the fish in the pond, the parts are limited in what they know. It's not just about embracing all parts of your vision. It's about going the distance with each of them. This is the key to manifesting your vision. Each part plays a crucial role, and you need all of them on board to make your vision a reality.

Embrace them, for they are the steppingstones to a fulfilling life and manifesting your vision.

Parts Choosing a different Belief.

I have manifested my vision alongside these parts, and I believe each part holds the power I need to manifest my vision. Each part goes the distance with me when:

- Each part chooses a different belief.
- Each part decides how it wants to show up. Each part transforms into its highest version.
- Each part changes its role.
- Each part returns to its original state of being.

You are not just shifting your beliefs but empowering yourself by understanding and approaching them differently. You are not eliminating or overcoming them. Instead, you are developing an understanding of them and addressing their highest needs.

Going the distance with no parts left behind means you learn to validate these parts and recognize their experiences. Remember, you co-wrote your story.

Why are you so hard on these parts? Why are you focused on eliminating them? These parts co- wrote your story, and removing part of the story eliminates parts of you.

Remember, you are the co-author of your story. Every part, every experience, is embedded in it. These parts co-wrote your story, and you need to acknowledge them with importance and relevance. Each part of your story is significant and deserves to be understood and appreciated, just as you deserve to be treated with importance, relevance, and appreciation.

To eliminate a part is to eliminate a part of yourself that has shaped you and made you who you are today. Embrace these parts, for they are integral to your being.

Instead of dismissing these parts, honour them for what they have done. You are here today because of these parts. Reflect on your choices; you will notice the parts that influenced the decisions that brought you to this point in your journey.

These parts served a purpose, guiding you through difficult situations and leading you away from danger, unfulfilling relationships, and stale jobs. They always prioritized your safety and well-being.

It's all about the approach and changing your perception of these parts. When you do, you reach a place where you can say, "I am resilient because I made courageous decisions that influenced my choices, even when I was scared." These parts helped you take a leap of faith.

It's about shifting your approach and changing how you communicate with these parts. In the past, you have used negative, disempowering language and engaged in actions that degraded these parts. You mistreated them and caused pain, though not consciously; the parts that wanted to keep you safe stepped in.

It's time to grant yourself the freedom to embrace compassion and forgiveness, allowing them to flow through you.

Like a fish in a pond, you don't know what you don't know. You have been conditioned to act and think in a certain way and believe your actions are correct.

Instead of reacting impulsively, you can respond with mindfulness. Instead of holding grudges, you can practice forgiveness. I invite you to explore these new approaches with openness and curiosity. Be ready to be amazed; this process will surprise you with its impact. You will be amazed at what you uncover. I promise you that.

Mastering Self-communication and Building Trust with the Parts.

The pain of fear holds multiple parts of beliefs. When you experience fear, the gatekeepers shield and protect you from feeling the pain. Protective parts come to the rescue, and layers of belief parts take over to protect the fear part from emotional harm.

What can you do when this happens?

Learn to communicate—develop a conversation and communicate with the parts in the language they know best. Mastering self-communication is not just a skill; it's the key to unlocking potential relationships with the parts. It's about creating a dialogue with the different parts, each in a language they understand best.

Trust-building is a mutual process. You must realize that these parts also need to build trust with you. They need to know they can trust you once you develop the language and learn to communicate with them. It's a shared responsibility. This understanding is crucial in building trust with the parts.

Trust is like a fragile bridge in a relationship. When someone repeatedly hurts you, that bridge breaks. Rebuilding it becomes daunting as you tread a path of distrust to shield your heart from further pain. Trust, in this context, is the tool you use to build a relationship with the parts. If trust is not established, the gatekeepers will keep the parts at a safe distance.

Trust is the key. These parts need to trust us. They need to believe that we will hold a safe space and be there for them when they reveal their pain. This trust will bring them closer to us, enabling them to communicate, share, and open. Trust is not just important; it's the cornerstone of building healthy, strong relationships. And for us to establish a healthy relationship with these parts, they must trust us.

With a heavy heart, we need to acknowledge why these parts have lost trust in us. We have a history of neglecting and avoiding these parts, even trying to eliminate them from our lives. We haven't included them in our vision or acknowledged and validated them. We've ridiculed and judged them, not believing in their capacity to transform. Instead of empowering them, we've disempowered them. These actions have led to the loss of trust.

Consider this: how can these parts trust you when all you've done is break and tear them apart? It's a question that demands self-reflection and a commitment to change.

Reflecting on these actions is crucial to understanding how they affect trust in relationships. You have tried to eliminate these parts in everything you do, yet you expect to manifest your vision and become your highest self when none of these parts are on board.

Who do I need to be rather than what do I need to do? It's about understanding and working with these parts in harmony to embody every aspect of your being.

Moment of Reflection

CHAPTER FOUR
Parts are Co-Authors of Our Story

You can't erase your story by distancing yourself from past experiences.

Have you ever considered the stories we tell ourselves? It's interesting how our experiences shape our beliefs and emotions, becoming part of our personal narratives. Without realizing it, we may spend most of our time trying to eliminate parts of our lives based on these stories. These beliefs feel real because they are the result of our conditioning. However, it's important to remember that we have the power to rewrite our stories. We are the authors of our own narratives, and we can create a new vision for ourselves that aligns with our true desires and aspirations.

It's not always easy. You will face resistance from past narratives. But with awareness and self-belief, you can go the distance, face these challenges and rewrite your story.

Your life is shaped by the story you tell yourself. Every decision you make, every action you take, and even every inaction is influenced by this story. Over time, you begin to identify with this story and believe it is your identity. Your story is like a fish in a pond, limited by what it has access to.

Similarly, the beliefs and perspectives you may hold will limit your authentic story.

These limitations shape your thoughts, beliefs, emotions, and ultimately, your daily actions. The co-authors of your story play a significant role in shaping it. These co-authors are the characters that contribute to your story, like your family, friends, and experiences. They have influenced your thinking and impacted your life, whether positively or negatively.

If you understand that these co-authors have shaped your story, you can take control of your narrative and create a more empowering story. By recognizing their influence, you can identify limiting beliefs and embrace new perspectives to help achieve your goals.

Consider this: every experience and part of your journey has led you here. You may have pushed some parts aside to move forward without acknowledging them, but they shouldn't be dismissed. They are co-authors of your story and excluding them is a mistake. Take a moment to reflect on them, understand their role, and accept them as part of your unique story.

You are not alone in writing your story but are in a partnership with these parts. You capture each other's essence and create a vision you all desire. Approaching these parts' struggles and limiting beliefs with curiosity can change your perspective. Instead of trying to eliminate or suppress these parts, embrace them as co-authors of your story. By understanding and acknowledging them, you can see how they contribute to your life's narrative. This perspective shift can help you transform limitations into superpowers and possibilities for growth.

Let me guide you through developing a new healthy relationship with these parts from the lenses of curiosity, and you will notice everything shifting.

I reflect on some of the emotions I have experienced and how they may have influenced my story. It's important to acknowledge that emotions like shame, guilt, loneliness, and fear are powerful co-authors that shape how we perceive and remember our experiences. As I explored further, I uncovered parts that held onto rejection and abandonment. I invite you to reflect on your experiences: what emotions or beliefs have shaped your story?

You may have tried to rewrite your story by ignoring or suppressing the emotions and parts that hold them. But it's important to recognize that every part of your story has value and deserves acknowledgment, even the painful or uncomfortable ones.

Can you erase these parts from your story? Can you rewrite your story without them playing a role?

Let's explore creating a new version of your story that includes these parts. What would that mean for your narrative?

How do you rewrite your story without including its co-authors? How did you get here in the first place? You didn't write this story alone, just as you didn't get here alone.

This book emerged once these parts felt certain and transitioned. When they became certain, I trusted the process and moved forward without leaving any parts behind.

These parts, which I call the different aspects of your personality, co-authored your story with you. Thinking you can move forward without acknowledging these parts is a mistake. Saying, "I'm rewriting a better version of my story, and you're dismissed," is a mistake. What happens when we approach these parts that way? They resist.

You send a harmful message when you try to disengage from parts that have experienced abandonment or rejection. You imply they are unwanted, unvalued, and unimportant. This can lead to internal conflict and hinder your growth and ability to achieve your vision.

When you approach these parts with understanding, you realize they are reliving past pain. If they experienced rejection or abandonment, that has shaped your story and become part of your narrative. By disengaging from these parts, you are not just rejecting them; you are rejecting yourself.

Ignoring these parts means dismissing yourself. Every time you try to eliminate these parts, you invalidate your own experiences. It takes courage to develop a relationship with the co-authors of your story. You have the power to rewrite your narrative, but it requires true understanding to accept all parts of yourself, even the ones you may not be proud of.

Embrace these parts, as they are part of your unique story. By accepting them, you accept all of yourself, even the difficult parts. You and I don't have the power to eliminate these parts. I invite you to explore this with me. Remember, we are not alone in this struggle; these parts are with us, too. It's a shared journey of self-discovery and acceptance.

Have you considered the harm we cause when we try to eliminate these parts? What if the part holds beliefs around rejection and abandonment? The message we send is that they are irrelevant, rejected, and abandoned. This can lead to internal conflict, self-doubt, lack of self-acceptance, and feelings of unworthiness, hindering personal growth and happiness. How can we manifest our vision with disempowered and dejected parts?

We can't eliminate the parts we see as limiting. Instead, we can explore and understand why we hold onto them. What if we approached these parts with compassion and curiosity instead of rejection? These parts were rejected in the past and are now rejected by us again. The parts that feel rejection also feel abandonment.

They are reminded daily of their insignificance or lack of value, which is very painful. When we reject these parts, we create more pain, stopping us from reaching our life goals. So, instead of trying to eliminate these parts, let's embrace and understand them. With compassion and acceptance, we can heal and transform these parts into a powerful force.

Every time you try to eliminate these parts, you are rejecting parts of yourself. By doing so, you are abandoning parts of yourself that have already experienced abandonment. As you strive towards your goals and vision, remember that embracing these parts helps relieve early painful experiences. Each effort to accept them is a step closer to healing.

The key to creating a life of your design is simple: don't try to eliminate any parts. It's not about erasing or ignoring them but embracing them all. That's the crucial first step on your journey. Remember, you aim to move forward with no parts left behind.

As you read these chapters, pay attention to what arises within you. Take a moment to observe what's happening, accept it without judgment, and acknowledge your feelings, thoughts, emotions, and sensations. These parts can transform their pain into healing when they are accepted and validated. Take comfort in rewriting your story. Remember, you are not doing this alone; you're going the distance with these parts as you rewrite your story.

Moment of Reflection

CHAPTER FIVE
Rewriting your Story with Parts

When rewriting your story, do it with certainty.

These parts determine what their best version looks like and what beliefs they need to have to achieve their desires and connect to their true selves.

Think about your life story that you've been creating. Do you want to keep living this story, or is there a part you want to change? Take a moment to think about which parts of your story you like and which parts you want to rewrite.

Doing this helps you take control of your story and create the life you really want.

Time for self-reflection.

It's important to take a step back and ask yourself some key questions about the stories you tell yourself.

One question is: what part of this story is working against my vision? Think about what you truly want to achieve and whether your story helps or hinders that vision.

Another question to ask is: what part of this story doesn't align with my soul's desire? Your soul knows what truly resonates with you. If your story doesn't match your soul's desires, it might be time to re-evaluate it.

You might also ask: what part of this story doesn't represent me? The stories we tell ourselves shape our identity. If your story doesn't reflect who you are, it's important to reassess it.

Finally, consider: what part of this story doesn't show my authentic self? Your authentic self is your truest version. If your story doesn't reflect that, it may be time to rewrite it to align with your true self.

Before setting goals and creating your vision, it's important to ask yourself these powerful questions. They can help you identify the parts of your story you want to change. For example, ask yourself which part of your story you want to focus on and improve. Starting a conversation with these parts can help you gain clarity and direction towards your goals.

Feel free to use this process.

I encourage you to engage with parts of yourself. Recognize each part's role and express your desire to rewrite your story with their help.

If you're thinking about rewriting your story, understand that you don't have to do this alone. I strongly suggest you engage and communicate with all parts, ensuring none are left out. You can start by saying, "I'm ready to rewrite my story and need your help." By working with all parts, you can create a different narrative that truly reflects your goals and who you want to be. Remember, the journey may feel unfamiliar and scary, but with the support of all the parts, you can achieve the life you desire.

Focus on each part and validate them. One way to do this is by saying, "I understand you learned to protect me and the purpose it served. You've helped me understand you better. The conditions and circumstances led you to develop this limiting belief. I get it. Help me understand your true desires so I can help you achieve them."

Change the approach.

You have worked hard to become the best version of yourself and achieve your goals. However, certain fears and limiting beliefs can sometimes hold you back. Instead of blaming these parts for your setbacks, try to understand them. Remember, the aim of these parts is to protect you. By acknowledging and validating them, you can move towards achieving your grand vision and living a fulfilling life.

Let's take a moment to reflect. Are you saying that to become your highest self, you must eliminate all the parts that have shaped your life's story? The question is, will your new story be complete without these parts?

You become complete when you embrace and align with all the parts. Recognize that you are a culmination of all your parts. You are one with them, and you can rewrite your story only when these parts know they belong. So, you must let go of the idea of eliminating any parts. That's the first step in going the distance. Moving forward means you are on this journey together; you are co-authors of your story, which is incomplete without these parts.

Getting all the parts on board is crucial to achieving your desired results and bringing your vision to life. This means changing how you approach these parts and working to reconcile your relationship with them. Trying to eliminate these parts will only slow your progress and take you further from your goals.

So, focus your energy on moving forward with all parts, leaving none behind.

Have you ever wondered why you seem further from manifesting your vision? Here's why. My biggest revelation was discovering the many aspects of these parts and their potential to transform. I also learned that eliminating or rejecting these parts led to unfavourable outcomes.

The 'parts' I'm referring to are different aspects of your personality, beliefs, and experiences that make up who you are. The part that wants to eliminate any part is also a part of your personality, beliefs, and experiences. You co-create with these parts all the time, and you may not be aware of it.

That's why you find yourself stuck in the same patterns, like a fish in a pond confined to a familiar and limited environment, not yet experiencing the vast possibilities. The same goes for the parts.

These 'parts' only know what they know—they function with the same information, recreating the same outcomes by retelling the same stories. For instance, you have a 'fear part' that always tries to keep you safe by avoiding risks. On the other hand, you might have a 'courage part' that pushes you to take bold steps. So, when you feel the urge to drive fear away, that's the gatekeeper part' trying to disengage from the 'fear part,' and for a good reason.

Anytime we strive for progress and change, we will encounter resistance. When we try to push through this resistance and change our lives, these parts become anxious and feel threatened. They are like fish in a pond, safe and secure in their familiar environment.

These parts are comfortable where they are. However, it is important to acknowledge that these parts also seek to fill a void, one that needs to be met with compassion and understanding. Instead of ignoring or suppressing them, we can create a safe and supportive space for them as we work towards our vision.

By doing this, we can help these parts feel heard and validated, ultimately achieving a greater sense of peace within ourselves. As you create a safe path, these parts can return to their original state without leaving any part behind. This is what they truly desire—to reconnect with their true essence, a state they may not know how to reach. Your role is to guide and help them on this transformative journey.

Reflecting on my journey, I've learned how important it is to connect with these parts. This has made them feel safe, heard, and understood.

Creating a safe space for these parts to move forward is crucial. They need to feel secure and assured that they won't be left behind. This is a space where their emotions, feelings, and beliefs are acknowledged, deeply valued, and validated.

It's important to understand that the current state of these parts isn't their true nature. Even if they seem wounded or damaged, their real essence is in their unaltered, authentic state. From your early experiences, these parts took on a role to protect you. Initially, you were in a state of authenticity, not driven by survival.

Your coping mechanisms, formed from past experiences, have shaped your current feelings, emotions, and beliefs. These experiences have caused these parts to operate in survival mode, a stark contrast to their original state. Even now, these parts are driven by a strong need to keep you safe and protected. Remember, reconnecting with these parts means reconnecting with your authentic self.

It's important to accept these parts as the first step towards creating a safe path for them. Instead of seeing them as limitations, we need to embrace them as they are.

This process creates room for healing, freedom, abundance, and creativity.

The journey inspired me to dig deeper and connect with these parts. I have discovered a breakthrough process that has transformed these parts. This process can revolutionize and transform your life in unexpected ways.

These parts only know the past; they don't experience the present or future. They appear in your daily life, still stuck in the past. That's why you find it hard to move forward; these parts affect your daily life, making you feel like you're hitting an invisible wall.

Have you ever felt unable to move forward?

You are stuck with parts from the past, and they only know the past.

But here's the key: to change the past, start by acknowledging the parts holding on to it. This isn't just a step; it's crucial for future growth and transformation. By acknowledging, empowering, and transforming these parts, you're helping these parts move forward.

Trying to ignore or get rid of these parts is exhausting and won't work; it only leads to more frustration, disappointment, and suffering. Denying them a place in your goals and vision will hinder your progress. But here's the exciting part: engaging with these parts can turn them into steppingstones and fuel your vision. By doing this, you can break through the invisible wall and reach your full potential. Embrace these parts as necessary for your journey and let them propel you forward. The potential for transformation should inspire you to engage with these parts.

When you say to these parts, I can do it all by myself. I don't need you.

That's a big mistake.

Acknowledging all these parts, even the ones you think you don't need, is crucial. Recognize that you are a sum of these parts, and they all contribute to your unique identity.

Thinking you don't need them is a big lie. You will continue to suffer until you recognize that these parts co-wrote your story and brought you this far.

Why is creating a safe space for these parts necessary?

There's a process to this process.

First, these parts need to feel your acceptance and assurance. They need to know you won't abandon them. When they feel safe, they will become their true, free selves.

Let's recognize that these parts have unconsciously shaped your beliefs for most of your life.

The beliefs you hold protect and keep you safe.

So, until these parts feel you are safe, they will keep trying to protect you. This might show up as self- sabotage, limiting beliefs, doubts, and fear.

All these parts act unconsciously, thinking they are protecting you. You'll keep hitting the invisible wall until you create a safe space for these parts to feel secure and move forward.

Where do you begin, and how do you establish a safe passage for these parts?

As part of the process, these parts need to know it's safe to go the distance. You can't just say it; you need to create a space where they can feel safe while moving forward. If you want to achieve your vision, you must create a safe path for these parts to join you. Otherwise, you'll keep hitting the invisible wall. These parts will only be part of your big vision if they are certain, it's safe to go the distance.

Once these parts feel safe going the distance, they will reveal the truth of their fears or limitations. This is when you create a safe space—a container to hold what is being revealed and expressed. That's when the path starts to open. For these parts to move forward, they need to know you won't abandon or leave them behind.

These parts need to feel valued. To do that, you must first share your big vision with them. You need to communicate your vision to these parts. This process has helped me understand myself and my parts better, and why I struggled to achieve my vision. The breakthroughs since then have changed how I approach my goals and vision.

Remember, pursuing your vision means stepping out of your comfort zone. This can cause uncertainty and fear because these parts seek safety, and fear creates uncertainty, making the comfort of familiarity feel threatened.

However, when we invite these parts to see our vision as already manifested, the response is different. There is nothing to fear when we experience our vision coming true, which can create a sense of safety, certainty, and relief. So, it's crucial to share our vision with them. When we don't share our desires with them, they feel unimportant and unvalued. So, let's include all parts when pursuing our dreams and visions.

Every time you create your big vision and don't share it with these parts, you dismiss them. What you're saying to these parts is, "You don't matter." To go further, what if one of these parts has experienced abandonment before? By excluding them from your vision, you're telling them it's time to step away again.

To create a safe and supportive environment for all parts, it's important to recognize that each part serves a role and helps shape your story. Each part can contribute to achieving your big vision and plays a vital role in making it come true.

This is when you step in and engage with these parts. You need to share your vision with them if you want to move forward without leaving any parts behind. Communicating your epic vision to these parts is essential so they are on board with your plan. This will ensure alignment in achieving your vision as you embark on the transformational journey, going the distance with no parts left behind.

The following chapter will explore how to create a safe passage when communicating your vision with the parts.

Moment of Reflection

_____

_____

_____

_____

_____

_____

_____

_____

_____

_____

_____

_____

_____

_____

_____

_____

CHAPTER SIX
Safely Connecting with the Parts

Fear is a natural part of this process, and by acknowledging it, you can begin to address it and create a path for transformation.

It's important to understand that when these parts don't see the vision you want for them and yourself, it triggers fear.

Firstly, validate and acknowledge these parts. Then, invite them to experience the vision you have manifested. Let them feel what it's like to be free from the burdens they hold so dear and see what is possible so they can fulfill their vision. They need to fulfill their voids. These parts will define what they need while immersed in the vision.

Why? These parts don't have to work so hard to protect you. They know you are safe, and they are safe, as there's no fear of the unknown because these parts see the vision as manifested. They recognize the potential for transformation. The experience aims to invoke growth as the parts transform.

Once these parts have experienced your vision for them and yourself, they will naturally seek to fulfill a need and desire. This is a natural response and a sign that the parts are progressing in transitioning and transforming their beliefs. Be open to the process and embrace them as they transition.

Look for evidence in your life of the belief parts, such as "I'm not good enough," "I always mess things up," or "I'm not deserving of success." Then, ask yourself: What do I believe to be true for myself? Take a moment to reflect on your beliefs.

Then, question those beliefs. Are they true? Or are they old beliefs formed in your childhood or past experiences you've been holding onto? The beliefs you currently hold shape your actions and decisions.

For example, do you genuinely believe you're not smart or capable enough? Or is this just an old belief formed in response to a difficult situation? Challenge the original belief as your adult self. By questioning and challenging these beliefs, you gain a deeper understanding of the thoughts that hold you back. This self-awareness is the first step toward personal growth and transformation.

Is it possible that, from that experience, these parts believed they were abandoned because they were unworthy and thought they were unloved?

Now that we have the history of the belief part, we, as the adult self, can separate ourselves from these parts while also acknowledging the experiences of the child self and these beliefs as true for those parts.

When you establish a deep connection with different layers of these parts, they feel heard, seen, understood, and, most importantly, safe with you. You need to create a safe space for these parts. They need to know they are safe enough to go the distance.

It was an experience that altered a part of you, and to this day, these parts feel compelled to protect you.

I share what I discovered below, which will revolutionize your relationship with them.

Parts' early experience and history

Your experience, which may have originated from a situation you perceived as unloving or unworthy, has shaped you. You developed beliefs from past experiences that stirred emotions of sadness, anger, and guilt. These parts, born from your early experiences, are not weaknesses but survival mechanisms showing your resilience and strength.

Their role is to protect and keep you safe. Their original state of being was pure and authentic.

While working on emotions and beliefs is important, I've realized it's not the only solution for achieving the results I desire. Through my personal journey, I've experienced the transformative power of working on emotions and limiting beliefs.

My healing journey revealed that reclaiming and liberating the parts is challenging and requires exploring different approaches. I managed to empower some parts that were trapped in the past, but I still struggled with others. I used various methods to heal the wounds and free the parts, but I often found myself agitated, triggered, and limited.

Then, I had a breakthrough. I discovered a method that revolutionized the process, opening new possibilities for healing and liberation.

My Aha—-hitting the invisible wall.

Realizing the limiting belief parts limited my capacity to manifest my vision: It didn't matter how many programs I took or courses I invested in; I still hit an invisible wall. I was doing the work, digging deep into different healing methods, and overcoming limiting beliefs, but I was still hitting the invisible wall.

I continued working on my unconscious and conscious limiting beliefs, yet I still faced the same barrier. I was going the distance but was further away from manifesting my vision.

I also learned the power of visualization and meditation. What an experience! I was connecting to my body and mind, yet I once again hit the invisible wall. Manifesting my vision was becoming impossible.

I know I'm not alone in this. You, too, may have invested time, money, and energy into self- discovery, healing, and personal development. You've focused on your vision and created a plan for your dreams and aspirations.

The great news is that you can live the life you desire. Consider it done, as everything you envision is already here. I will share the process of going the distance with no parts left behind and breaking through the wall once and for all.

These parts hold emotions and beliefs. Other parts will open when they feel safe, understood, validated and acknowledged. The first step is getting past the protector of these parts, the gatekeeper.

As I share, you may relate to these parts. Take time to get to know them. I recognize it's hard work; self-work takes time. Through healing, I've been able to connect to these unconscious parts, including abandonment and rejection.

These are parts I've come to know very well. These parts have been present most of my life. With their help, I embraced a new approach that transformed their beliefs. I am grateful for this new perspective, which has opened a world of healing possibilities.

Before writing this book, I attended to some of my wounded parts. I've done a lot of healing, yet I would still get triggered when certain situations or memories brought up feelings of abandonment or rejection. Despite all the self-work, I wondered why these parts had not healed. It was an incomplete puzzle I was determined to solve. Little did I know that the feelings of abandonment or rejection were experiences my child-self went through.

Abandonment and rejection

Separating beliefs and emotions

I don't want to dismiss the experience these parts are holding onto. It's important to be clear: abandonment and rejection are beliefs, not emotions. A belief is a perception, while an emotion is a feeling.

I was waiting for my daughter in the parking lot. I had called her in advance, but despite this, she took her time coming to pick up the food I was delivering. I noticed my mind running wild with thoughts. Surely, she doesn't appreciate you. You've taken your time to deliver this food to her, yet she doesn't value what you do for her. It means nothing to her. It's not important enough. You are not important enough.

All these beliefs started showing up. Then, of course, the emotions followed. I found myself getting angry, and my voice rose—all while sitting in the car for five minutes. It felt like the longest five minutes. Then, my daughter finally showed up, smiling, and I kept thinking, "Can you imagine the audacity? She's finally showing up, all smiles!"

You can imagine my look, as I was really upset! After all, she didn't value me, so I felt I wasn't important enough. All these thoughts and emotions in just five minutes are the parts of the beliefs feeding on each other. The stories you tell yourself in silence are driven by these parts.

All these layers of beliefs were coming from a part I know well—the abandoned part. It's a good thing my daughter noticed my mood and said nothing. Eventually, I realized what was happening and did what I always do: attune and attend to these parts.

When I called my daughter, she said she knew what part that was. We've had many conversations about these parts; I thanked her for not saying anything and letting me and the part be. I have invested a lot of time in inner self-work, which has opened me up to a higher level of understanding and helped me recognize the parts holding onto the wounded beliefs of rejection and abandonment based on child self experiences.

As the adult self, I recognized the experience as valid for the young self, not for the adult self. Separating the experience is very important. I'll share more: I was unaware of these parts until I started doing the inner work. I didn't know these parts existed, yet they appeared at different stages of my life. I noticed the patterns.

I will share how I shifted my belief around rejection and abandonment. But before I do that, I want to talk about these parts of abandonment and rejection and see if you recognize them in your life: I had created a vision that I wanted to manifest but noticed resistance. I did everything possible but kept hitting an invisible wall. I didn't understand why. The beliefs you hold onto are based on past experiences; they're not beliefs you suddenly wake up with today. These belief parts have shaped you from a very young age, like a story co-written from your experiences in difficult or uncomfortable situations.

The belief may come from a place of unmet need. Maybe the need was to feel loved and attended to in the way you wanted, and it didn't happen. It doesn't have to be a dramatic experience, but it can be a big deal for a child. The belief part may be that I didn't get the love and attention I needed, and the story may be that I was unloved and unwanted. Self-awareness is the key to recognizing our triggers, and it's a crucial step towards healing and wholeness.

We get triggered all the time, and most of the time, we don't even realize it. Especially when it comes to relationships, my go-to place is bringing awareness of emotions and beliefs and exploring them with curiosity. Often, I recognize it is familiar to me; this feeling and belief predate this moment. By doing so without invalidating my experience, I can focus on myself more and attend to my feelings and beliefs with compassion and understanding rather than victimhood. I focus on what is happening to me. It's crucial to be gentle and forgiving with ourselves; practicing self-compassion in these moments creates room for growth and healing.

Moment of Reflection

CHAPTER SEVEN
The Origin of Parts

"Trauma is not what happens to you; it is what happens inside of you as a result of what happens to you."
-Gabor Maté

Your body is a complex system that instinctively knows how to protect you. During difficult times, these parts developed different beliefs to keep you safe and alive. Remember, even if these beliefs limit you now, they were crucial in keeping you safe in the past. Sadness, anger, and fear are trapped emotions

Here's what I discovered: These parts use information from the past, which is the only information they have. This information is outdated and doesn't serve them or us. Like a fish in a pond, you're stuck with old information that needs upgrading.

Imagine how these beliefs show up in your adult life. Anytime you are triggered, these beliefs will appear, and other parts of you will step in to protect you from getting hurt. Notice when that happens. These parts will come to the rescue by disconnecting or feeling compelled to fix or please. These are the stories you co-created with these parts.

How can you transform these parts? If there's one key takeaway from this book, it's this: get to know your parts. By understanding their role in your life, you'll see how they shape your experiences.

Like a bird in a cage, knowing it has the potential to soar but confined by the bars of its current circumstances. These parts don't realize they're trapped and that they can access more.

It's time to liberate these parts so they can access the abundance available. This doesn't mean you invalidate their experiences. If you want these parts to access new information, which they don't currently have, you must help them.

When you approach these parts with compassion, curiosity, and understanding, you will recognize their power in your life.

These parts occupy significant space and have a strong hold on you. It's important to understand that these parts are there to serve, protect, and keep you safe. They played a significant role in your life, especially during the earlier stages when you were helpless and needed them.

As an adult, these parts, still stuck with the same outdated information, continue to protect you even when you don't need protection. This is because they have become automatic responses. However, as an adult, you are no longer helpless. You can recognize and challenge these outdated beliefs and behaviours.

These parts don't know the difference. It's your role to show them that you can care for yourself and don't need their protection. You can reverse the role, as these parts need you as much as you need them.

Now, you want to take back control. But you cannot do it by eliminating these parts, as it won't work that way. The gatekeepers will stand guard to protect the parts from getting hurt.

These parts protect you. They step in whenever they detect unease, discomfort, or uncertainty. To understand them better, we must explore their origins.

My birth experience.

I'm very familiar with the abandoned parts. Where did these parts come from?

My mother became very ill when she was eight months pregnant with me. She went to the hospital and was put on bed rest for a month before delivering me. At the time, my mother had high blood pressure and swollen feet; she could barely walk, and her condition was uncertain. The doctors worried for my mother and the unborn child. They were unsure of the impact my mother's health condition would have on the baby. My father and grandmother stayed at the hospital with my mother, sharing the doctors' concerns.

The doctors were concerned about the survival of the baby and could not guarantee that the child would be born healthy and alive. My father, a man of faith, told the doctors, "I put my trust in God and will continue to pray for both my wife and my child."

After a long month in the hospital, my mother went into labour. Unfortunately, her health condition had worsened. During labour, she was going in and out of consciousness. By the time I was delivered, my mother had passed out and was unconscious, unaware of my condition as a new baby and not knowing whether I was even alive.

Let's take a step back for a moment.

Imagine you have this unborn child in the womb, and the mother is in and out of consciousness. Can you imagine what is happening in the womb?

Consider the stress levels the mother is enduring, her concerns for her unborn child, and the physiological changes in her body. The unborn child feels all of these experiences in the womb. Remember, this is the first place you call home, a sanctuary where safety, comfort, warmth, and love are first experienced. The womb is your first home, a shared space of profound safety.

You may not consciously remember what happens in the womb, but your body does. It holds the memory of the experience, and that memory can manifest in various ways in your life today. The parts you are talking about stem from those memories trapped in your body, a phenomenon known as "body memory."

If you have ever experienced an unsettling situation, your body will remember. Your body is that sophisticated. It will hold on to the memory until you unlock it.

My first experience of uncertainty started in the womb. The safety in the womb shattered, creating a fear of not knowing if I would make it. This uncertainty was my first experience, and it created a trapped memory critical to establishing a sense of safety. Certainty is connected to safety. When I am certain, I feel safe. When I am safe, I am certain I can get through anything. This has shaped my entire life.

I will share more in other chapters, and you will begin to realize the connection.

You will recall that my mother was unconscious when she delivered me. Going back to the first time I entered my second home; my mother was unconscious.

Imagine being a first-time parent who just delivered your firstborn child. You are unconscious, unaware if your newborn is even alive, let alone healthy.

What is the first thing a newborn need? What is the first thing a mother does with her newborn? When a newborn comes into the world, it seeks comfort, connection, and safety.

Now, imagine that with my mother unconscious, the doctors were still attending to her while the nurses rushed to my rescue, uncertain if I would make it. Imagine the experience of the newborn entering the world with uncertainty.

When the nurses took me to my grandmother, she was amazed I was still breathing. My grandmother, whom I call Ayeyo, was scared to hold my tiny, fragile body. I was so small I could barely fit in her palms. The blood pressure had sapped the life out of me.

I can't imagine how my Ayeyo felt with two lives at stake. In one room, her daughter was in critical condition, and in the other, her grandchild's fate was uncertain. The nurses placed me in a glass container, likely an incubator, in a dark room alone.

How did these parts shape the beliefs and the stories?

Now, let's keep exploring how these different parts developed. Uncertainty in the womb breaks the sense of safety.

Let's look at the experiences of the newborn. I will use the term "newborn" to honour the inner child's experience, as this is not something I recall as an adult. It was my inner child's experience, and telling the story through that lens is essential.

I share using my inner child's voice.

The safety of my first home was shattered and uncertain. I entered my second home longing for warmth, to be held, comforted, and assured I was safe.

Remember, the baby does not know or understand the adult world and, therefore, does not grasp that my mother is not well. The experience of the newborn is different from that of the mother. My mother was unconscious and unable to hold and comfort her newborn.

I entered a world where I was not accepted, held, or received with warmth. There was no one to hold me, no connection. I was left alone in a dark, cold room.

Now, imagine what this experience might be like for the newborn.

Let's unpack the parts that can impact the newborn's experiences. Let's return to Gabor's quote: "It's not what happens to us; it's what happens inside of us that will shape our beliefs around the experience." That is the memory that trauma holds. It's not what happened; it's how we experience the events.

I've shared the events that happened. Now, let's unpack this deeper.

My inner-child self-experiences.

Uncertainty came when the safety of the womb was shattered. When I entered my second home, my mother was not in a condition to hold and receive me, leaving me feeling unloved. This made me unconsciously believe that I was unwanted and unloved.

I was placed in a dark room alone and left in a cold place, which made me feel unwanted, unloved, and unworthy. The big revelation is that the experience of being left alone creates a sense of abandonment and rejection. This revealed another part: since I was rejected and abandoned, it meant my existence was not valued.

My father later shared that my birth was nothing short of a miracle and named me Fadhwa, which means "a miracle." It was a miracle; my mother and I were released from the hospital two months later; we both survived the ordeal and survived miraculously.

Now consider the harrowing flow of unconscious emotions a newborn experience:

- The overwhelming waves of sadness
- The fiery bursts of anger
- The chilling grip of fear
- The isolating depths of loneliness

The longing for safety, a feeling that many of us understand, was not readily available. This was not a natural experience for the newborn. Although not chosen on purpose, these stories are important because they form unconsciously.

They are not beliefs you pick; they are the results of challenging situations and how you interpret those experiences. Understanding these unconscious beliefs is a key step toward acceptance and healing..

I unconsciously held emotions and beliefs hidden from my conscious mind. When I started doing inner work, these parts came to light, and I found the trapped memories and beliefs held in my body. I learned that I could release these trapped emotions by changing my beliefs. That's why it's important to leave no parts behind.

The belief part keeps the emotions safe. Until these beliefs trust that you can handle the emotions, they will keep doing what they know best. A story was written before you were born, and the chapters continued to evolve. Your role today is to rewrite the story. You can only do this when these parts agree to change. Remember, their information is outdated and no longer serves you or them.

I will go deeper in the following chapters.

I ask you to be open, think about your experiences, and look into your early memories. Some clues will give you more information to help you understand these parts better and see how they shaped your beliefs today.

I know people who have done this work and understand the experiences of the inner child and even the time in the womb. They know trauma can start in the womb. Some may ask, how can a baby experience trauma in the womb?

A baby can experience trauma in the womb. This can happen if the mother carries generational trauma, if the father or mother's genetics carry trauma, or if the mother is in a stressful and fearful environment. This stress is passed on to the baby, showing that the health of the womb affects the baby's health.

Here's a story courtesy of these parts that I unconsciously co-wrote with and would like to share:

> *Nobody wants me. Nobody loves me. I'm unloved. I'm not wanted.*
> *This place is not safe. It's uncertain.*
> *They don't want me—they have not accepted me.*
> *I cannot receive love from this place; therefore, love is unavailable.*
> *I am abandoned; they have rejected me, and I'm not wanted.*

The gatekeepers and co-author's perception of the experience is narrating the story.

> *She feels abandoned and rejected; we don't want her to feel sad, alone, or scared.*

> *She thinks that because no one welcomed and held her, she does not matter. She feels irrelevant and that her existence does not matter.*

The gatekeeper begins to assign roles: These are the parts that come to the rescue.

> *We will make her feel valued by meeting her needs with the help of the fixer, pleaser, and perfectionist.*

Gatekeeper parts come in different ways.

> *The compulsion to be good, to be on your best behaviour:*

> *You're not going to cry, so they won't leave us alone. You're not going to make a fuss.*

> *You're going to be good. You're going to avoid rejection.*

You're going to be a people-pleaser. You're going to be the fixer and fix things. You're going to make up for the loss. You're going to suppress and not say anything! These parts fulfill a need and fill the void that came from the experience.

Notice when these beliefs resurface in your present moment, and remember these beliefs predate this moment.

These parts come to our rescue—the gatekeeper's step in to protect the wounded parts, keeping you safe and alive. Next, we will explore the origin of fear and its impact on our daily lives.

Moment of Reflection

CHAPTER EIGHT
Understanding the Origin of Fear

When these fears resurface, remember that they stem from your past, existing long before this moment.

I had not known that my experience in the womb had lifelong impacts, including an unexplained fear of drowning. Every time I stepped into a large pool or approached the beach, a primal fear gripped me. Being in the water felt like a menacing force, ready to engulf me.

It was a revelation that fear could be linked to our earliest experiences. I realized that my fear of water was rooted in the memory of being in the womb, where I was surrounded by fluid. This understanding helped me approach fear with more compassion and understanding. Fear was a memory trapped in my body, a memory from an early experience that began in the womb.

What should I do next? My old belief was to get rid of the fear. How did I do it? I knew nothing about swimming apart from the videos I watched on YouTube.

My strategy for conquering fear was to confront it head-on. If the fear was drowning, I would immerse myself in the water and not let myself drown. I might not have known how to swim, but I was determined to eliminate this fear.

The fear of drowning was intense, but the life jacket provided a sense of security that allowed me to venture into the water. As I dog paddled in the pool, I felt both fear and determination. My primary goal was to conquer the fear, and learning to swim was secondary. I knew that to swim, I first needed to feel comfortable in the water, and this realization fueled me.

Of course, I managed to float in the water with my life jacket on. I paddled from the shallow to the deep end. I was excited; I finally rid myself of the fear of drowning.

I know swimming alone without a lifeguard is risky, especially at 5 a.m. What if something happened? What was I thinking? True, I had put myself in danger. I think I depended too much on the life jacket, but it did keep me afloat and safe.

I wasn't aiming to become an expert swimmer. What I truly wanted was to conquer the fear of drowning and feel at ease in the water. And I did. I realized the water wasn't the obstacle; it was the fear.

As I spent more time in the water, I began to feel safe and confident. I had overcome the fear of drowning. I was comfortable enough to be in the water without constant worry. It was a significant milestone.

I discovered that being in the water with a life jacket differed from being in the water without one. It was a revelation, and I realized I was not yet ready to remove the life jacket, even in the shallow end; I was not safe. The life jacket was a safety net, keeping me afloat and secure. But without it, the fear of drowning resurfaced, reminding me once again that I was not safe in the water.

Even though I was more comfortable in the water, the fear of drowning was real. Realizing I needed to learn to swim, I enrolled at a local community centre with exclusive slots for women's swimming classes, creating a safe and supportive environment.

The instructor gave me a waist belt the first time I walked in. I relied on the waist belt for the first three sessions. I was on a mission to conquer the fear of drowning. I was ready, eager, and focused to dive into the pool. In the back of my mind, I told myself it's just water; you can do this.

During the sessions, I became confident, energized, and ready to hit the water. I felt like the next Michael Phelps, a pro with the belt on. I attended every class. Every Sunday, I was first in line, ready to go like a great student.

With every stroke, all I thought was, I will not drown, I will not drown. After three sessions, the instructor finally told me to remove the belt. Everything I knew and learned about swimming flew out the window when I removed the belt. The fear of drowning was crippling. It didn't matter what the instructor said, her words seemed slow: *Lift your knees—lift your knees—it will help.*

Interestingly, I heard the instructor's words, yet my body wasn't connecting to what she was saying. Parts of my body disconnected from the rest. My mind understood what was said, but my lower body didn't register it. The disconnection was alarming. I could hear the words again, lift your knees, yet my lower body was not getting the message. I found myself facing my worst fear—drowning, as the water was overtaking me.

As the instructor pulled me above water, I wanted to stop because of the sheer embarrassment—a grown woman who cannot swim, what a shame. I noticed my self-judgment. As I looked around, admiring women who, despite their fear, kept going back to the pool,

I asked myself, how can I stop now? I'm here to get rid of this fear. I want to enjoy swimming and love being in the water.

Knee-deep in the water, there was no going back. I came so far and was not about to let fear hold me back. Exhausted after a couple of tryouts, I took a break and stood by the side of the pool.

Despite the fatigue and the fear still lingering, I felt a spark of determination within me. It was then that the instructor called me, sensing my struggle and wanting me to succeed.

I paddled back to the pool. Here's how my conversation went in the pool without the safety belt on.

"I'm going to be here," the instructor said.

"You can't leave."

"No, I am not leaving. I'm here."

"Okay," I said. I asked if she could stand in front of me as I swam towards her.

We tried that way. While making sure her fingertips were close to mine, I knew she was not far from me. I knew she was right there, and I swam wonderfully. To my amazement, I was fine, and I swam further and further.

I was able to lift my knees and stand up. The instructor was standing right there with me. She never left. I didn't experience the fear of drowning, either. Then, she encouraged me to repeat the same. So, I swam towards her, and our fingertips gently touched. It gave me comfort to know I would not drown. She was right there.

"I'm going to stand aside," she finally said. "I am right here. I'm not going anywhere. I'm right here with you. I want you to do what you've been doing. You got this."

She was more confident than I was.

I went. Then, the paralyzing fear of drowning returned. What just happened? I wondered. The instructor came to my rescue and lifted me above the knee-deep water.

I kept thinking, what is going on?

I've done a lot of work on myself regarding that time.

With curiosity, I started asking myself, what am I missing here? The initial fear was a fear of drowning, yet something else was coming up that I needed to explore and investigate further.

Drowning experience

I asked myself, why is it that when my instructor stands in front of me, I'm doing great? I can swim, and I know what to do. Yet the moment she steps aside, the fear of drowning comes back. When she stands in front of me, the fear of drowning goes away.

I stood there and reflected on the experience. And then it hit me. I realized that knowing she was there, in front of me, created a sense of safety. Her presence made me feel safe, like she was there to hold me. That comforted me. It was a reassurance that she was there for me. At that moment, I realized, wow, I was familiar with seeking comfort and safety.

I did not realize the fear of drowning had multiple layers. The drowning was one layer. The next layer was the sense of comfort, knowing she was there, making it a safe experience. Then, the fear kicked in because the next layer was the feeling of being left alone when the instructor stepped aside. This brought up feelings of abandonment. Now, this opens a whole different experience.

The safety is gone; I am alone, abandoned, and scared, with no one to rescue me. I am drowning; this environment is not safe.

The threat to safety activates multiple layers of these parts. Everything is connected. It wasn't just the fear of drowning. The fear of drowning was the gatekeeper.

The gatekeeper keeps everything locked up until there's a safe passage for them.

Consider this: the beliefs are not just thoughts; they didn't just pop into your head one morning. No, these beliefs are ancient, deeply rooted in your being, and have shaped your life since your earliest memories. Each belief is a co-creation, born from the experiences that shaped you. If you yearned for love and attention in your childhood, a story was woven around this experience, creating a belief you internalized as truth. This understanding validates your journey, and you embody the belief—believing it is true.

You co-created your life story with different parts, experiences, and personality traits, and that's why you cannot move forward without these essential parts. You may think you can rewrite your life story on your own, but you need to realize that the story you are rewriting needs to be told from your highest self, not from where you are today. This process involves reflecting on your past, understanding your present, and envisioning your future, all from a perspective of growth and transformation.

You are a co-creator; to rewrite your story, you need to be in harmony with these parts. You can only change your story when you are in alignment with them. For instance, you cannot eliminate your past experiences, personality traits, or values, as if you're trying to get rid of a part of yourself.

Ever wonder why you sometimes find yourself further from your vision and your dreams seem impossible to achieve? Ever wonder why? Here's why. I'm not speaking only from my experience; I know this is true for many.

I have noticed that in pursuit of your dreams and desires, you are simultaneously working on overcoming fear, self-sabotage, and limiting beliefs. This process can delay your pursuit of manifesting your desires. You put emphasis, attention, and focus on mastering these limiting beliefs in attempts to eliminate them.

Remember, these beliefs are also parts of your experiences. Therefore, whenever I mention parts, I am talking about beliefs you may hold that are still driving your decisions and results.

You are setting yourself back as long as you pour your energy into eliminating these parts of your beliefs. The more you do that, the further you are from achieving your vision. Every time you try to eliminate these parts, you are sending a message to them.

Let's say my focus is to eliminate fear. My energy is focused on removing these fears; thus, I have set myself up for greater fear. The more attention, focus, and energy you put toward eliminating your fears, overcoming limiting beliefs, self-sabotage, or procrastination, the further away you are from your vision. Your vision is no longer your reality. You are working so hard to eliminate these parts, but these parts are what got you this far.

The stories you've been telling yourself have been with you your whole life. These parts co-wrote your stories. Different parts of your earlier experiences co-wrote your stories. These parts are co-authors of your story. If you say you are going to dismiss and eliminate them, you are telling these parts that you are done with them, that you are writing a new story, and they are not part of it.

You are saying that none of these parts are relevant to your story. What happens when you take that approach?

Let me paint a clear picture of these parts' conversation with you. It's not just a conversation; it's a power struggle, with each part vying for control of the narrative.

> It goes like this:
> *Do you think you can you eliminate us?*
> *Do you think you can go the distance without us?*
> *Do you think you have more control over your life than us?*
> *Can you rewrite your story without us?*
> *Do you think you have the power and control to dismiss us?*
> *We will remind you that we are the co-authors of your story.*

It's crucial to recognize the role and value these parts, such as your emotions, thoughts, and experiences, have in your life, even if they don't seem to add value now.

Dismissing them could mean they continue to live in your story, potentially leading to unaddressed issues or unfulfilled potential.

These parts will put up a fight, making it hard, if not impossible, to manifest your vision. So, what then? How do you achieve your epic vision? Let's be clear: you can't manifest your vision without these parts because it's a holistic journey. Going the distance means no parts are left behind. Some may argue, "But I don't want these limiting beliefs!" You might believe that these limiting beliefs are to blame and are your enemy.

Some may even say, "It's because of these limiting beliefs that my life is a mess, my health is deteriorating, my business is not growing, and my confidence is low. These parts are slowing me down and have prevented me from achieving my goals. Life is difficult with these beliefs, and I don't want them." I understand why you feel this way; I did, too. If there is another way, would you be open to considering it? If so, let's go deeper.

Now, I urge you to try to understand these parts with curiosity, from their perspective. You've focused on eliminating these parts, which is why you have difficulty manifesting your life vision, goals, and objectives. You are further from your vision whenever you engage in dismissive behaviours and minimize these parts. It's crucial to understand that you don't have the power to eradicate any of these parts. Accepting this truth is the first step towards growth.

I encourage you to observe when you direct your energy and focus toward ignoring or avoiding these parts. Is it a compulsion to eliminate them? Take note of this. These beliefs can restrict your ability to achieve your goals and your soul's desires. I invite you to recognize that the current process is not producing the desired results. Doing so inadvertently creates a disconnect within yourself, which distances you from manifesting your vision. You hold the power to change this.

Here's a gem I discovered: The further you are from manifesting your vision, the safer these parts are and the stronger they are at holding you back. But remember, within you lies a strength that can overcome these barriers. You're causing yourself more damage than you think. So, I urgently invite you to notice this.

As you start a transformative journey, take a new approach by being open, curious, compassionate, understanding, and willing to explore. By challenging your limits and embracing new possibilities, this shift in perspective can unlock the door to manifesting your vision, leading to a future filled with growth, fulfillment, and transformation.

I am sharing this with you because I have personally experienced it. I am amazed at the potential for growth and transformation. This process has not only worked for me but has also transformed the lives of many of my clients. The good news is that it's not just me who can benefit; you can also transform those parts of you that have held you back and kept you limited.

This process is accessible to everyone. To begin, you need to explore one part at a time. It's a journey that starts with a single step. Ask yourself which belief parts you would like to explore in your current state. Once you have a safe passage and those parts have evolved and transitioned, you can invite others. Work with one part at a time, as these parts have layers.

Every part has its desires, and every part is essential. Not leaving any parts behind means that every part influences, defines, and shapes the vision you intend to manifest.

Every part's unique desires are essential. "No parts left behind" means that each part has a role in influencing, defining, and shaping the vision you want to manifest. Each part, in its own way, contributes to your grand vision. These parts are not just contributors but co-authors of your vision and narrative. It's important to remember that you are living a story that shapes your vision and approach to life. In this narrative, it's easy to forget that it wasn't solely your efforts that brought you here; you couldn't have reached this point alone. I want to acknowledge the parts that have contributed to manifesting this vision. I didn't do it alone, and I didn't get here alone.

Throughout my journey, I recognize that each part plays a pivotal role in breathing life into my vision. It's not just about acknowledging and recognizing these parts but also about appreciating their unique contributions.

Acknowledging my highest version that continues to show up, evolve, and challenge me—the highest version that is not a passive observer but an active, dynamic, constant co-creator of the vision I aspire to manifest, shaping my identity.

To manifest my vision, I must delve deeper, identifying the beliefs and emotions that drive each part. I also need to address any limiting beliefs that hinder the manifestation of my vision. What about the parts that hold beliefs that are still in captivity?

What about the beliefs that limited your imagination?

What about the beliefs that hold onto fear? What role do they play in all these different parts? "No parts left behind" means every part goes the distance.

You may be saying, "Hold on a minute. I've spent time, money, focus, and attention on overcoming and eliminating fear, and you're telling me I am taking the fear part with me?"

My response is simple: The process is not about eliminating fear or limiting beliefs. It also does not mean you are taking these parts in their limited form. The process is to transform the fear and the limiting parts. No parts left behind means no parts left behind.

The belief that holds the fear also holds different versions of fear. Remember, every part that goes the distance has its own story. In that story, there is a vision it seeks to manifest. This includes the part that holds the fear of fear and uncertainty. These parts have their vision.

Just imagine the transformation when these parts change. When you transform the fears of uncertainty, failure, and the unknown, imagine the possibilities that await. To reach your highest potential, you must transform these fears into their highest versions, with each fear showing up as its best self. You want these fears to tap into their potential as well.

These fears need to know that you are not leaving them behind.

If you feel stuck and unable to move forward or far from manifesting your dreams, it may be because you have spent most of your life trying to eliminate these fears. As long as you've focused on eliminating these parts, you will experience limitations. By doing so, you are inflicting pain on these parts and further harming yourself every time you try to eliminate them.

The harm in doing so is sending a message to these parts. You are telling them they are irrelevant and don't matter. Instead, imagine the potential for growth and self-acceptance when you communicate with them, acknowledging their relevance and importance.

One of the biggest problems is that when you try to uproot and eliminate these parts, you are saying, "You're of no use to us, no longer needed here." That is the damaging message you send whenever you try to eliminate them.

How can you find your highest version of yourself when you say no to these parts? How can you achieve inner peace while suppressing a part of yourself? And how can you bring your vision to reality when you deny your true self? Rejecting a part leads to self-rejection, and self-rejection hinders self-acceptance, growth, and healing.

How do you say yes to yourself when you have said no to parts of yourself? How can you ever align with your vision when you are not aligned with yourself?

These are important reflections to consider. Be honest and intentional during the process. Remember, saying no to a part of yourself means dismissing a vital part of you. Minimizing a part of yourself can hinder your ability to achieve your epic vision. So, ask yourself, what happens when you say no yourself? How can you expect to reach your goals if you're not embracing all parts of who you are?

How do you accept and receive your epic vision? You do it by expecting to receive the abundance waiting for you. How can you expect to receive abundance when you haven't accepted it within yourself? And how can you manifest your epic vision when these parts have not transitioned or transformed? Instead of eliminating these parts, how can you create space for them? How do you expect to find wholeness from the absence of these parts?

You now know that going the distance means leaving no parts behind. You also understand you can rewrite a new version of your story, but you cannot do it alone. You need these parts that co-wrote your story. Therefore, to rewrite it, you need them as they are co-authors of your story. Your story will only shift once you realize these critical pieces.

To rewrite your story, you must understand and accept all the parts. You can only transform your story when you acknowledge every part. Ignoring parts of your story won't work, as each part has a unique story and meaning that contribute to your overall story. By eliminating certain parts, you are erasing a part of your history. Instead, you should work with all parts of your story and redefine their meaning.

This is where true transformation happens; only then can you move forward in harmony with your story. For this to work, you must be on the same page with all parts of yourself. Otherwise, you will be further away from your highest potential and from manifesting your vision. How can you be whole when you hold onto the wounded parts of yourself? Remember that you live in a story that continues to replay in your life, which you have co-created based on past situations. But you can rewrite the narrative and create a different story. Otherwise, these parts will continue to hold you back and limit your ability to move forward.

These parts are like the bars of a cage that keep the bird safe and protected. The bird stays in the cage because it's familiar and feels secure; that's all it knows. It's the sense of familiarity that keeps it there. Similarly, these parts are comfortable with familiarity, and any uncertainty creates discomfort. These parts will close the bars to keep you safe.

Have you ever found yourself unexpectedly overwhelmed by emotions from the past, even during a harmless event? You're not alone. Sometimes, situations trigger emotional or cognitive patterns formed in response to past traumas or significant events. This phenomenon, known as triggering, can leave you uncertain or confused. For some, it's more than just a brief discomfort; it can be deeply unsettling, making the world feel unsafe.

When unresolved parts are triggered, your emotional reaction might range from hurt to fear, rejection, or abandonment. For instance, you might feel hurt or rejected if someone cancels your plans, even for a valid reason. You could also feel a surge of fear when a particular object or sound reminds you of a past traumatic event.

This mix of thoughts and emotions is something we all experience. But here's the empowering part: you can learn to manage your emotions and heal from past traumas by becoming aware of and understanding these triggers.

Imagine a butterfly trying to fly out of a jar only to find it can't. In the same way, we can't escape difficult situations by simply trying harder. Instead, we need to create an environment that allows us to grow. Trying to overcome limitations by cutting off parts of ourselves is pointless. Just as the butterfly can't fly out of the jar into the open sky, we can't escape our limitations by denying parts of who we are. We need to create space for growth and expansion.

You can't eliminate these parts. Instead, you can develop an understanding of them.

Moments of reflection

What do these parts believe to be true for them? What limiting parts still hold you back? I know mine all too well. What are yours? Is this familiar?

I'm not good enough. I'm not worthy enough.

I'm not deserving enough. I'm not beautiful enough. I'm not smart enough. I'm unworthy of love.

What about the parts that show up as people-pleasing, perfectionism, or trying to fix everything? Or the parts that make you disconnect, detach, or avoid things? Think about the parts that aren't always obvious but still affect your emotions. What do you feel when these parts are triggered? Fear, guilt, shame, anger, sadness, anxiety, or maybe numbness?

Now, imagine the energy it takes to keep these beliefs going and the space they occupy inside you. What if you used that same energy to transform these parts? How would your life change if you redirected this energy towards positive transformation?

Think about the immense potential within you, the vast space waiting to be filled. Imagine a life where you use this power to transform these parts for your benefit, not against you. How different would your life be? Use that same energy force to explore the possibilities of moving forward with no parts left behind. Discover the path this journey may take you. I invite you to be open and curious, allowing self-exploration to begin. Approach the unconscious parts with awareness and understanding.

Fear of Being Alone

The fear of being alone, deeply rooted in beliefs about rejection and abandonment, often drives our thoughts, feelings, and actions. We may struggle with this without even realizing it. We feel compelled to be perfect, to fix things, and to please others. We might not notice when we silence our voices to maintain relationships out of fear of being alone. But now, I have come to a profound realization. I recognize the countless times I silenced my voice and minimized my own needs out of fear of being alone. This was not a conscious choice; an unconscious belief drove me to think that if I spoke, I would be rejected, abandoned, and left alone. Therefore, I stayed silent and suppressed my feelings, believing it must be my fault and that I needed to fix it. This understanding has inspired me to deeply reflect on my actions and their roots in my unconscious beliefs, and I hope it can inspire you too.

It's only now, in hindsight, that I can see how deeply my unconscious beliefs shaped my choices, decisions, emotions, and behavior. In moments of conflict, I would fall silent, feeling an overwhelming urge to mend the situation while burying my emotions. I would put on a facade, disregarding my feelings and needs, all in a desperate attempt to salvage the relationship, even if it meant muting my voice.

It's painful to realize that I was sacrificing my feelings to restore normalcy. I failed to see that by suppressing my emotions and stifling my voice, I was perpetrating an injustice upon myself. I believed the issues were my responsibility to fix, so I ignored my feelings and pretended everything was fine. My desperate attempts to salvage the relationship only served to worsen the situation. The silence and the compulsion to fix and please didn't lead to a resolution; instead, they only deepened the injustice by suppressing my feelings and neglecting my needs.

This cycle continued for days—pleading, fixing, and pleasing but nothing worked. In the end, I was left alone, sitting in silence. Realizing that all my efforts made no difference left me numb, shocked, and in a state of utter confusion.

I found myself in a solitary battle, an intense struggle that consumed me. My insignificance was crushing, and the battle I was fighting felt like a heavy burden that I couldn't shake off.

My efforts were in vain, as he left despite my desperate pleas, attempts to fix, and compulsion to please. I was left rejected and alone; the weight of rejection weighed heavy on my heart, my suppressed emotions now running wild feelings I could not control.

I started bleeding profusely, fearing I was having a miscarriage, and went to the emergency room. After tests and blood work, the Doctor concluded that the bleeding was a sign of a recent traumatic event. As I lay in the hospital bed, the realization hit me like a wave. The emotions I had been trying to suppress were so overwhelming that they had to find a way out of my body.

It has been a profound realization that my compulsion to fix things to please others was rooted in a fear of being alone. Even more surprising was that this fear had been with me long before that moment.

Moment of Reflection

CHAPTER NINE
My Story: How It Started

Realizing the key to going the distance.

I recently found out that these parts had layers I needed to understand. I discovered these layers as they changed and transformed during a safe passage.

The parts that came out during this safe passage were those of abandonment and rejection. These parts, which I knew well from my healing journey, became the foundation of my self- understanding.

During a meditation session on December 26, 2023, I envisioned my grand vision. This transformative moment sparked the creation of this book and its subtitle, 'No parts left behind'.

I've written many books that are stored on my iCloud, but this one felt urgent and needed to be released immediately. The revelation I experienced will help you liberate your parts and speed up your progress toward manifesting your vision and living the life your soul desires.

Despite investing a lot of time, energy, and money in programs, learning, and unlearning, I felt further from my goals. It seemed like there was an invisible wall I couldn't get past. We all struggle to navigate life, often feeling confined by an invisible barrier. However, I've discovered a breakthrough that can free us from these limits.

This discovery, which can break through the invisible wall and help you achieve your epic vision, has been a game-changer for me. Despite trying many life-enhancing programs, none revealed what I'm about to share with you.

I'm about to reveal a secret that might be the first of its kind. Its potential for personal growth and empowerment is inspiring.

I'm going to share a simple yet powerful approach that can be applied to all areas of your life. As you use this process, you'll see positive changes in the areas you focus on and in your overall life.

Remember, this process covers all aspects of your life and isn't limited to any specific situation. It will transform your life and help you achieve your goals.

When you commit your time, money, resources, and energy to realizing your grand vision, it's crucial not to overlook and leave any parts behind. If you face challenges on your path, take a moment to pause and reflect. This self-reflection is a powerful tool that can help you identify what is holding you back from achieving your goals and manifesting your vision.

What is preventing you from achieving your soul's desire? What is preventing you from creating the life you desire? You've probably been told how gifted you are. You have a special gift. Maybe you know it, or maybe you don't, but believe me, you do. No one can duplicate the gift you hold. Remember, there is only one of you in this world.

I, too, have had people remind me of my gift. They would ask, "What's going on? Why are you hiding behind a podcast? Why are you hiding behind a YouTube channel? Why are you not out there?"

I could never answer because I was plagued with self-doubt. I questioned the value of my voice, my message, and my ability to make a difference. This uncertainty kept me from stepping out and sharing my gifts with the world.

These well-meaning voices would say, "You have so much to offer. You have miraculous gifts; you have impacted lives. We see that you can achieve your vision. This face, this voice, and this message need to reach people." Yet, their words, though meant to inspire, only deepened my self-doubt.

I thoroughly reviewed my vision, goals, and dreams, and realized most of them were still unfinished. Seeing that I was far from my vision and that my passion for inspiring others had faded was eye-opening. The creative projects that once fueled my spirit had all stopped, leaving behind a void.

Instead of focusing on completing these goals, I kept spending more money, time, and energy on more courses, programs, and certifications.

I'm not saying investing in a program is bad; I learned a lot. However, there may be a disconnect that you might not be aware of.

I didn't realize there was still a piece missing. I invested a lot of time in healing, understanding myself deeply, and getting to know myself better than ever. I was doing inner work and becoming aware of these parts of myself. I understood my emotions, beliefs, thoughts, and behaviour patterns well. I learned to understand different emotions and beliefs and how to communicate with and listen to them.

I recognized the importance of self-reflection and discovered the power of pausing, quieting down, and contemplating my emotions and thoughts. Doing this made me more mindful and aware of my feelings and beliefs. I worked on addressing emotions like sadness, fear, shame, and anger. I also challenged beliefs that I was not good enough, inadequate, or not smart enough, which were rooted in my past experiences.

I delved deeper into the origins of these emotions and beliefs. This process required patience, compassion, and understanding. I could understand and heal them. Over time, I created a safe space where these parts of me felt validated and accepted.

These parts didn't have to look outside for what they needed. Through self-awareness and understanding, I could provide them with what they needed. This realization empowered them, making them feel capable and in control.

These parts no longer had the compulsion to please, fix, or be perfect. They were accepted as they were. There's nothing to fix. Accepting and loving these parts liberated them from seeking approval or striving for perfection.

The parts were accepted and reassured, making them feel at ease. By fostering self-acceptance, I guided them to a place of liberation where they no longer needed to fill a void or doubt their worth. Let these parts be heard, validate their experiences, communicate with them, and show them what is possible.

I discovered the missing piece, inspired by the book's subtitle title: No Parts Left Behind. Have you ever wondered why you are still far from achieving your vision?

Even though you have done the inner work, gained knowledge, and set your goals, you might still wonder what is holding you back.

I had the same questions, wondering what was holding me back despite coaching clients and seeing miracles in their lives. My vision was at a standstill, and I often found myself hitting an invisible wall again.

Moment of Reflection

CHAPTER TEN
Clarity on Your Vision

Approach your vision as if it has already manifested.

Beware of the stories you believe that don't align with your highest self. These stories can block you from achieving your epic vision.

Know that your highest self is not a distant dream but a reality. Your journey now is to raise your understanding to this higher level. The vision you aspire to is not just a wish but a reality already here, ready to be manifested.

With greater understanding, ask yourself, "What actions do I need to take to make this vision a reality?"

Remember, everything in your life is interconnected. This holistic approach is your strength.

How do you experience your big vision? This is how my vision shows up:

The vision my soul desires comes to me easily, effortlessly, abundantly, and faster than I expected.

Why? Because I'm coming from a place of abundance that already exists.

I'm manifesting my vision from this place of abundance, where all parts of me and my highest self are connected.

These parts and my highest self come from abundance, transformation, inspiration, healing, knowing, meaning, purpose, and certainty.

An unclear vision can leave us feeling uncertain and reveal gaps in the creative process. Imagine someone asking you to go with them without telling you where they are taking you. Would you agree to go without knowing the destination?

What would it take for you to decide? Would you follow someone mindlessly, even if they have no idea where they're going? To agree to accompany the person, you need to know where you're heading and trust the individual before making your decision.

No one follows someone blindly unless there is trust.

Now, let's apply this to our parts. We've been treating them the same way, so it's no wonder they resist. You're asking these parts to go the distance with you without explaining where you're going. Can you imagine the outcome?

I now understand the response: "Where are you taking me? How can I come with you when you haven't told me where we're going?"

I invite you to pause and reflect before moving forward. What part of this resonates with you? Notice and journal any insights or "Aha" moments you experience.

How can you expect these parts to trust your direction when it's unclear? How can they follow you without trust? And how can they follow you when you're not sure where you're heading?

Why would they leave their comfort and safety and blindly follow you into the unknown?

The struggle with fear of the unknown and uncertainty is a common thread that binds us. Understanding this is crucial: when your vision lacks clarity, it triggers the fear of uncertainty. Naturally, these parts of you are uncomfortable with venturing into unknown territory.

Unconsciously, these parts try to fill a void driven by fear. In doing so, they continue to feed on that fear based on old beliefs. These parts want to feel safe. When you ask them to follow you without a clear vision, it creates uncertainty and threatens their safety. You haven't established clarity in your vision or communicated it to these parts. They know how many times you've tried to eliminate them.

These parts will only trust your direction if your vision is clear. If there is uncertainty, they will resist. Remember, their role is to protect and keep you safe. By resisting, they slow down your progress, and you find yourself facing another invisible wall.

You must establish a clear vision and communicate it with these parts. Build trust with them, showing that you are not trying to eliminate them but are going the distance together, with no parts left behind.

Now you realize you haven't been clear about your vision and haven't communicated it with these parts. You also see that by trying to eliminate these parts, you've triggered fear of uncertainty and the unknown.

When these parts are in fear mode, they resist change, compromising safety. When there's resistance, you find yourself hitting the invisible wall, further from manifesting your vision. These parts inspired the next revelation I'm about to share, so I give full credit to them. They played a crucial role in a revolutionary breakthrough moment. If a part's history is connected to a belief around abandonment or rejection, that part will naturally seek safety and comfort and resist the unknown and uncertainty.

I have discovered a way to revolutionize your life and help you achieve your epic vision.

Have you considered not eliminating certain parts of your life but instead clearly communicating your vision and including those parts? Doing this lets you achieve your vision without leaving any parts behind.

Let's forget about "how" for now and stay open to other possibilities. You may have tried different options before, but now it's time to be amazed by a new experience. Going the distance without leaving any parts behind means you co-create your vision with all the parts and your highest version. In the following chapter, we go over what you need to start crafting your epic vision..

Moment of Reflection

CHAPTER ELEVEN
Crafting your Vision

Your epic vision is your GPS, and your highest version is the anchor of your soul.

What if you approached your vision so clearly that you could see the finish line? What if you saw your 'highest versions', the best versions of yourself at each stage of life, as part of a relay, passing the baton, going the distance, and knowing when to pass the baton?

In this context, the 'finish line' is not a fixed point of achievement but a continuous process of personal growth and self- improvement. It's the journey that matters. The goal is to go the distance with no parts left behind, as each part and every version of yourself is a contributor.

You know when to slow down. If everything else is delayed, you stop, and the journey ends. To go the distance, you must let go of the need to be at the finish line yourself. As long as each version moves towards the finish line, you are going the distance. You are collaborating for each other's success, not competing against each other.

Learn to release control when you have reached your end and pass it on to the next version of yourself, who will also get you to the finish line. That's when you can anchor in your vision and, with clarity, know there's more of you that will get you to your vision. Why is this important? Your vision must be clear. Approaching your vision with clarity creates room for creativity and certainty.

There's a higher version of you ahead, closer to the finish line. Just because you haven't seen it yet doesn't mean it isn't there. Approach your vision with confidence and clarity. It's the life you want to create and live—your epic life.

So, who is creating this vision? Who is making this epic life happen? Who is writing your story? Can you see your epic vision?

The vision you're creating isn't just for you. These parts and your highest version are co- creator parts of this epic vision. You want to create, live, and enjoy an epic life. You want a life full of abundance that fulfills your soul's desires.

You need a clear vision to reach your goals without leaving any parts behind. That means going the distance with clarity.

You need a clear picture of the vision you want to manifest. This vision should come from a place of certainty, knowing you can achieve it. Look within yourself and let your highest version guide you towards the vision your soul desires.

Passing the Baton

I understand the frustration of coming so close to your goals yet feeling like you've hit an invisible wall. It's a common struggle that many have faced. You've tried creating a vision, setting goals, visualizing your success, and even making vision boards, but you keep hitting that invisible wall.

Think of it like a relay race, where each team member passes the baton to the next. Each player does their part, aligned with one vision, to reach the finish line. The first player doesn't cross the finish line, but they contribute by passing the baton. The next team member does the same, and with every baton passed, each team member contributes toward reaching the finish line. It's not about the last player who crosses the line but about each one completing their part.

In your personal growth journey, you're like a relay team, passing on your learnings, experiences, and wisdom to the next stage. Each stage contributes to the overall progress and eventual success.

Now, envision yourself in the relay, not just as a team member but as the many versions of you— each version passing the baton to the next. Each version of you moves closer to the finish line, contributing to the journey's completion. This is your personal relay, showing the contributions of each version of yourself.

It's not about who crosses the finish line last; it's about each version contributing to the finish. With each pass of the "baton", you trust you will reach the finish line because each version relies on the other. Your highest version is the culmination of your growth and evolution.

You reach a point where you must let the next version of you go the distance. Each version will help you get to the finish line. Each version knows when to stop and pass the baton so the next can take over.

With each passing, you find your anchor and witness your highest version, your ultimate potential, going the distance.

Create a vision you desire.

Think about all areas of your life and assess them. Then, ask yourself: What parts of my life need change? What needs improvement? What needs a quick transformation?

Is it your wealth, career, or overall health, including your mental and emotional well-being? What do you want to focus on? Is it a love relationship? Be clear.

Write a statement of the timeline when your vision has manifested:

> On this date _____on or before I have achieved _____.

> You want to create and design your vision as if it has already happened. Here's how to do it:

> Set a date for when you will manifest your vision. For example:

> "On this day, I am so happy and grateful. Love is abundant."

> If it's about wealth: "I am filled with an abundance of wealth."

> Write down the specific amount you want.

> "On or before this day, I have manifested $."

> "I am so happy and grateful for the wealth that continues to flow into my life."

Think about how your life will change. Add emotions to your vision. How is your life different?

How has manifesting your vision transformed your life? How has it helped society?

Your first goal is usually a surface-level goal. Once you achieve it, go deeper. Create a bigger vision. If your goal was to manifest $200,000, how has this $200,000 changed your life? How has it changed your business?

How have you grown? Now, create a bigger vision, one so big it scares you.

To manifest your epic vision, you need the right knowledge to overcome the fear that comes with it. Think of it as taming a lion. You might be in trouble if you wake the lion without a plan. That's why it's crucial to go beyond surface-level goals, where comfort keeps you stuck. If you stay on the surface, you'll struggle to achieve your vision. So, dig deeper and challenge your comfort zone.

When you show you're ready to go through the process, the gatekeepers of comfort might resist or help you. You must work with all parts to manifest your vision. The next chapters cover this process.

You create your legacy by aligning your epic vision with your highest self.

Once you go through the process, you manifest your epic vision faster.

You may have spent a lot of time making a vision board. I did, too. This time, though, my approach was different. I created my vision after going through the process, which allowed me to go deeper. All parts, including your highest self, should be involved in creating the vision, going the distance without leaving any parts behind.

Many people create vision boards without fully understanding the process. When you design a vision board, you might be doing so from a place of limitations, like a fish in a pond. These parts are unaware of the abundance beyond their comfort zone. These limitations can hinder your vision.

You're asking these parts to leave their familiar territory, disrupting their comfort and security. But by going the distance without leaving any parts behind, you open yourself up to growth and possibilities.

Understanding this process is crucial for creating a vision board that reflects your true aspirations. These parts ensure your safety. They will go the distance when they feel secure but will retreat if they sense fear or discomfort. These fears act as barriers, preventing you from exploring new possibilities.

It's important to recognize that comfort zones provide security and familiarity; stepping outside the comfort zone makes it challenging. Resistance to change is normal. However, growth and new possibilities lie beyond these limits. Our limitations can hinder the creation of our grand vision. Understanding this is key to gaining clarity. You cannot create your grand vision from a place of resistance and limitations. The surface-level vision is the gatekeeper, and it's limited.

Unlocking your grand vision

To unlock this bigger vision, we must go beyond surface-level dreams and move past the gatekeepers of safety. This means tapping into our creativity and inner resources. As we go deeper, we connect with our true desires and create a meaningful vision.

This is where you explore your creativity and discover hidden inner resources. As you delve deeper, the reasons for your journey become clearer. You start to understand why this step is important and connect with your soul's desires. This process unfolds like a secret being revealed, leading you to create something that deeply resonates with your soul.

You're now beyond the surface level.

In the following chapters, you'll understand these parts, their roles, and how to have them work with you instead of against you. This involves self-reflection, acceptance, and conscious decision-making.

Moment of Reflection

CHAPTER TWELVE
Inviting the Parts to the Vision

You must create a safe passage to help these parts go the distance. Invite these parts and let them experience your vision as if it has already manifested.

This creative process involves envisioning your dream as if it has already manifested. These parts need to see what you have envisioned, created, and manifested. If they don't, it creates fear of the unknown.

Have you struggled with the fear of uncertainty, failure, and the unknown? This means you still need to communicate your vision with these parts.

This process goes beyond shifting beliefs and it empowers the parts to go the distance. It allows each part to engage in self-revolution.

The process is as follows:

Separate yourself from the parts. Understand that you don't fear the unknown, failure, or uncertainty. Instead, a part of you holds the fear.

When you approach the process this way, you can step back and recognize the fear for what it is. This helps you relieve yourself from carrying the weight of the fear and allows you to help these parts rewrite a different story around fear.

Going the distance with no parts left behind helps these parts choose their path forward. Through this process, they undergo revelation and self-transformation. When these parts shift their emotions and beliefs, they redefine their meaning. They do this themselves; you don't.

When you invite these parts to your vision as manifested, the parts are not only part of the vision but experience the vision as their own. Once these parts experience what you've created, you have also valued and accepted them as they are, recognizing their uniqueness and wanting them in your vision, life, and future.

Once these parts of your personality, experiences, and emotions see what you've created, you value and accept them as they are. You recognize their uniqueness and want them in your vision, life, and future.

You are not trying to eliminate or destroy them. You bring these parts along because you need each one and recognize that each has unique abilities. You are not just co-creating the vision but co-authoring a new chapter in your life, designing it uniquely.

These parts developed beliefs based on your past experiences. Now, you are creating a space for them to develop new beliefs based on the experiences you create. The environment you create for these parts is crucial.

Remember, your environment shaped these parts. You need to create an environment where they can develop new, positive beliefs about themselves and return to their original state. You are free from limitations once these parts are liberated from past experiences. You regain your power when these parts transform and shift their beliefs. Limiting beliefs from past experiences are replaced with empowering beliefs that will support you on your journey. These parts transition into superpowers, working with you in ways you didn't think possible.

You have dreams to manifest and desires to fulfill in all aspects of your life. These parts need to see the vision and experience its full manifestation as if it is already here.

Creating a safe passage is not just a step; it's a crucial foundation. It's a space where these parts can express themselves without judgment or fear. This safety allows them to open up about their deepest fears and beliefs. As you navigate this, you may uncover multiple layers of beliefs and emotions. The first layer might reveal initial fears, but deeper layers could bring forth other emotions.

Remember, the process is transformative. It's about changing the beliefs held by certain parts. As these parts evolve and transition, they can move to the next layer. This journey allows them to create different versions of themselves, design what they want to manifest and step into a new, empowered reality. Only then can these parts create their vision of what they want to manifest. They see it and can now redefine and change the beliefs they once held.

You want to validate and acknowledge the experiences, beliefs, and emotions of these parts. Create space for them. Communicate with them, knowing you have the certainty and experience of manifesting your vision. You've seen this is possible for you. What do you choose for yourself?

Validating the parts

Once you validate and acknowledge these parts, you must communicate with and approach them.

I acknowledge and validate your concerns. I understand why you feel uncertain and fearful about the unknown. Please help me understand why you believe going the distance is unsafe.

Establishing clear communication is essential so these parts feel safe enough to express their fears to you. They need to know they can trust you and that you have their best interests at heart.

Thank you for sharing your thoughts with me. I now understand your perspective.

These parts don't want to feel left behind and alone. When you talk to them, reassure them that they will be coming with you and that you won't abandon them, hence going the distance with no parts left behind.

Communicate to these parts, and say:

We have been co-creators of our life and co-writers of our stories. I will not do this alone; we are writing a new chapter together. You are an important part of my life and have a key role to play. When these parts recognize their relevance and importance, they feel seen, valued, and validated. This helps them realize they have something valuable to offer.

In response, they acknowledge your appreciation and feel valued by you.

"You value me - I mean something to you."

Once these parts recognize their truth, your validation helps build trust.

Creating a safe space validates their experiences and honours their process. You have established safety with these parts; you trust them with your vision and invite them to go the distance with you.

You invite them to release any limiting beliefs from the past.

You want these parts to explore deeper and choose which beliefs they want to embrace. They may choose an empowering belief or want to free themselves from past roles.

Parts Transforming

You are opening yourself to the moment, allowing the experience to guide you as transformation occurs. Take time to be amazed by the changes within you. Providing a safe passage for these parts creates a sense of safety that allows them to experience what they couldn't before. This release and feeling of liberation enable them to relinquish old beliefs and limitations.

Liberated parts also release their hold on you.

This step is crucial, as the liberated parts will align with your highest self, especially when you reconnect with them. The playful parts are curious about their creativity, while the silenced parts, often overlooked, will transform and return to their original state, reminding you of their importance.

As you embark on this journey of self-discovery, embracing your playful self, you'll witness a profound awakening. Your creativity and curiosity will be reignited, allowing your higher self to emerge. This process will be a revelation, uncovering new dimensions of your being, leading to a state of wholeness and a higher version of yourself.

You may notice a new sense of being as the parts transition and transform, connecting you to your highest self. When you fully embrace your true self, you radiate positivity and become a light to others. The parts that once held you back transform into superpower parts. They no longer weigh you down; they lift you up and elevate you. You align with these parts.

You will manifest your vision faster when you align these parts with your highest self. Each part is supercharged and helps manifest your grand vision.

My Conversations with the Parts

These talks are important if you want to welcome all parts to experience your vision, let them change, and break free from their limits.

I asked these parts:

What makes you feel unsure and scared? Their response:

> *"I'm afraid of not knowing what's ahead; I don't know where you're leading me. I've never been to the place you're taking me; You've never been there either."*

I recognize and understand the fear. I realized I hadn't explained my vision well to the parts, making them scared and uncertain. Now, I'm making sure the parts can see the vision without fear.

The story you tell yourself over and over has influenced your life and made a narrative that holds you back. I didn't realize I was telling the fear parts: I'm moving forward without you.

It hit me hard that I hadn't shared my vision with all the parts. So, the talk went like this. I told the fear of uncertainty:

> *You weren't part of my epic vision. I didn't realize that not sharing my vision made things uncertain. Asking you to go where neither of us has been scary. I noticed the fear of the unknown tightened its grip on me. Thank you for the wake-up call; the farther I was from you, the farther I was from making my vision real.*

This made it clear how vital it is to share my vision with all the parts.

The fear part replied: *"You haven't been there yourself; how can you take me to a place where you haven't been?"*

I replied to the parts: *You're right.*

Then I asked the parts: Would you be open if I showed you?

It's crucial to know clearly what you want to manifest. This clarity will make the uncertain parts feel safe and help turn their fear into strength.

When you welcome these parts into your vision, it's important to give them the experience they're looking for and guide the parts that hold the fear safely. This helps them change and grow.

When you bring them into your vision, you need to make sure they feel safe and get the experience they seek and desire. The uncertain parts need to be sure about your vision. Whether it's falling in love or starting a business, the parts scared of the unknown need to feel confident in your path.

These parts can only go so far with you unless they trust it's safe. But if you make them feel certain and help them let go of fear, they can go even farther.

Fear is limiting. Like a fish in a pond, it's limited in growth. It's accustomed to a familiar environment; it's comfortable with familiarity.

Fadhwa Yusuf

Moment of Reflection

CHAPTER THIRTEEN
My Process for Inviting Parts to the Vision

This process is meant to show the parts how important they are and how their journey shapes our vision. Their role isn't just big–it's crucial.

I welcomed these parts and said:
I didn't think of you when I created our epic vision. Now I see that the life I dream of is incomplete and missing something important: you. Would you like to join me in witnessing something extraordinary? I'd love to share our epic vision's transformative journey with you.

I continued:

You're a big part of this new phase in my life.

Please, come along; I'm here with you. I want you to see this amazing vision firsthand.

I'm not just showing it to you; I'm inviting you to witness it yourself. You're free to leave or stay—it's up to you.

Guess what happened?

We invite the parts to see our vision come true, something they haven't seen or felt before. When they step into it, they'll have a special experience. Each part enters the vision and sees it happen. It's a change that challenges old ideas and sparks curiosity.

When these parts really get into our vision, they understand it better and change in a big way.

You'll be surprised by how these parts react, just like I was. These parts responded to the experience.

The first response: "I feel safe here."

These parts got really into it and asked, "Is this what you've been creating?"

They said, "I like it here. It feels safe—haven't felt this safe in a long time."

These parts then said to me: Thank you for inviting us and bringing us with you.

I kept the conversation going, allowing these parts to let go and free themselves. They start to reveal themselves when they feel safe. And for this transformation to happen, they really need to feel safe.

I asked, What are you afraid of?

Their answer was powerful.

"I'm scared you'll leave me behind, forget about me, and I'll be all alone."

This fear is real and needs our attention.

I made space for these parts to let go and be free. They start to open when they feel safe, and that's when they can change, grow, and heal.

These parts are the gatekeepers of fear. They protect other parts. But as the parts transition, they start to let go of the fear or belief. This is a transformative moment. Once gripped by limitations, entering the unknown is no longer daunting and impossible. With certainty, the gatekeepers let go of their defence as the rest of the parts begin to evolve.

Once they feel safe, the parts holding onto fear start to feel secure. They let go of that fear as they transition and embrace the possibilities. That's when the gatekeepers start to relax, and the hidden parts resurface.

But as each layer comes off, there's a feeling of relief and freedom, promising a journey of transformation and growth.

It's the fear behind the fear, a deeper and more complicated layer that needs attention and healing.

This step is important and needs patience and understanding. We're going the distance, making sure no parts are left behind.

I realized the first fear wasn't just about uncertainty and not knowing. It went deeper, hidden and unknown to me. Underneath that fear was the fear of being left alone and abandoned again. This is how we unlock the trapped parts. They've found a safe way out now. Talking to these lonely and abandoned parts is crucial. It's important to let them know you won't leave them behind or abandon them.

These parts are experiences from the past.

Once the gatekeeper feels safe, it relaxes and lets its guard down.

It's important to recognize the parts past experiences. Remind them that this vision belongs to them, too, by bringing them into the vision. As they explore new possibilities, they can shape a vision that's unique to them, creating something new together. We know we couldn't do it without their help. They need to feel empowered, knowing they're not alone in creating the vision; we want them involved, and we value them.

This process is meant to show the parts how important they are and how their journey shapes the vision. Their role isn't just big—it's crucial.

These parts need to know they matter, and they're not alone in this journey.

What you're telling these parts is that they can actively join in shaping a different vision if they want to. You're writing your life's story together, creating the next chapter with them, and ensuring no one gets left behind. The message to the parts is: You're not just watching; you're actively part of this.

For the first time, there was a feeling of relief, and the response from these parts went like this:

> *"Do you appreciate me? Do you think I have something valuable to offer?"*

My reply: Absolutely. You mean a lot to me. You're valued and significant to me. You have something valuable to share, and I can't do this without you. I need you here with me.

At that moment, these parts started to change. Like fish in a pond that were once stuck, they seemed to discover a way to abundance and weren't held back anymore. It was amazing to see these parts go from feeling limited to feeling abundant, moving freely and effortlessly. The parts responded:

"We're freeing you from ourselves and no longer keeping you in a space that holds you back. We've stepped away from that space that kept you trapped. Instead, we're here to lift you up. We're here to raise you to your best self, unlocking your huge potential for growth."

At that moment, I felt an expansion. For the first time, something incredible was taking place. There was a sense of peace and calm; the expansion within me felt open. It was surreal, the most magical and incredible feeling I've ever felt; it was dream-like. I felt the heavy weight had been taken off my shoulders. It was the start of a new journey in my life, a new chapter I was writing with these transformed parts.

Now, these parts are like superpowers. Can you imagine having all these parts as superpowers?

And think about the incredible things you can create when you work together to bring your vision to life. These parts of the wounded inner child must feel important. Their existence matters, and we need to value them.

I remember so clearly when I felt that smile come through—when I felt peace in my body and this inner light shining bright:

The part's experience is, as such, a big relief. *"I feel like I belong. I matter. I'm seen. Thanks for noticing me. Thanks for welcoming me, thanks for embracing me, thanks for letting me join this journey, and thanks for not forgetting about me."*

Parts appreciating the vision.

> *"Now I understand, and as I look around, I see the vision you've made real: this is where I belong. You didn't forget about me in this vision; you brought me along on this journey with you, even after all I've done. You brought me here. You trust me. You still believe in me."*

This book's subtitle was influenced and inspired by that single experience—no parts left behind.

Inviting the parts to the vision
Exercise

Get comfortable, like in a chair or on a bed, so you can relax.

Take a moment and focus on your breath. Breathe in deep, and as you breathe out, feel yourself getting more relaxed. Now, let's invite in the parts that are holding you back; this could be the part that sabotages your progress, or procrastinates, or even the part that is afraid of failure or the unknown. By recognizing and understanding these parts, you can go past them.

Bring in one part at a time because they've got layers. The first layer is like a gatekeeper.

Ensure a safe passage has been established. Once the gatekeeper feels safe, it'll let the other parts come out and express themselves.

Listen attentively. Pay attention to your body. Let the emotions, feelings, and thoughts flow through you. Notice any sensations like tingles or tension and let them be present.

Remember, you must be clear about where you're headed and what your soul wants to do.

Notice these parts and ask them, "What do you want me to know?"

Then, invite these parts to join in on the epic vision you're working on. Ask them:

Would you be open to me showing you something?

Would you be willing to come and see the vision you're helping create?

Note: Keep in mind that you're creating space just like you did with the emotions. A safe space for these parts to rewrite their story. It's important for these parts to be part of that story because you can't change your story without them.

You're not just changing the beliefs of these parts; they're also rewriting their own story based on those beliefs. You're going beyond sharing your epic vision. You want these parts to feel that the vision has manifested. You want to show them what life is like when there are no limits and when you go the distance.

These parts are co-creators in your life. Their beliefs led to the outcomes you're seeing now. To change the outcomes and get what you desire, you need a new vision that's aligned with the knowledge and ideas that will get you the results you aspire to. You can't get different results if you stick to the outdated information and old beliefs that held you back. And for these parts to change, they've got to transform their beliefs and ways of being.

Moment of Reflection

CHAPTER FOURTEEN
The Invisible Parts

The journey of these parts,
what we resist is what we seek; it's our void.

O ver the past couple of years, I've heard people say to me, "Why hide behind a mic?"

"Why don't we see more of you? You've got a lot to give. You're sharing so much: your knowledge, your wisdom, your insights, and your gems. You've got it all—you've got everything going for you!"

This message isn't just for listening; it's for reaching out to lots of people worldwide and making their lives better.

For a while, I didn't know what to do. I kept wondering about the same thing, but I couldn't figure it out. It made me feel confused and unsure about myself.

Only recently did I start to understand why. I finally saw why I was hiding from others, and it all came down to fear. I've made progress with these parts and gotten to know them well. I am very familiar with these parts, and I invite you to pay attention to how they manifest in your everyday life, too.

The invisible, unconscious part speaks of the limelight.

This part really surprised and amazed me: The part approached me and said: *"I've tried so hard to keep you out of the spotlight and prevent you from tapping into your inner light. The light inside you scared me."*

It continued:

The part that held fear approached me and said, *"I've worked hard to dim your light and keep you out of the spotlight, not because I want to control you, but because I worry about your safety and happiness. I want to keep you safe, shield you from harm, and protect the brightness of your light. I see all the great things you're doing, and that scares me; I held you back because I didn't want you to get hurt. I didn't think being in the spotlight would be good for you. I thought people wouldn't see you or appreciate the value you bring. I really wanted you to stay hidden, away from people's eyes. I just wanted to protect you from judgment and rejection, keep you from getting hurt, and shield you from any pain. All I wanted was to keep you invisible. I didn't want you to feel the pain of being invisible; I was worried you'd feel insignificant.*

Here, we notice the fear is of being invisible and not valued.

What you resist is what you seek.

The invisible parts will share their experience when they feel safe enough to reveal themselves. This often occurs when they see other parts changing and transforming.

Remember, these parts are parts from the past.

These parts felt invisible and wanted to keep me hidden until it was safe to talk about the pain from past experiences.

It's empowering to observe and witness the process.

It all began with being curious and open:

At first, the parts resisted, so I wanted to understand why. I asked the part to share and talk. It turned out to be a younger version of myself. This might sound strange, but I encourage you to explore this process with curiosity, openness, and a willingness to let go of what you think you know. Let the process guide you.

In the end, it could free these parts and change your life. It took a while for these parts to open to me because they needed to feel safe. After all, I was talking to a younger part of myself. When this part showed up, it was my nine-year-old self talking and saying:

> *"You've brought the parts here. If you're going all the way and making the vision real, will I get what I want?"*

I told the young part that going the distance and not leaving any parts behind meant making their dream vision happen and doing things their way.

Then I invited the parts to share, what kind of life do you imagine for yourself?

> And the young part said: *"I want to be free. I want to run around and be myself. I want to feel like my carefree nine-year-*

old self. I want to be happy, have adventures, play, and, most importantly, be whoever I want to be."

Then I asked the gatekeeper to join the conversation and said, I get what you're saying, and it sounds great. Are you up for making your vision happen now? Do you want to see what it's like in the way you imagine it?

The answer was: *"Yes, I want to do that now."*

This is an important step, going through a safe passage, a significant moment toward transformation.

I invited the gatekeepers who had already transformed to witness the parts change and transform. Their presence helped the younger parts feel safe and not alone, which was crucial in creating a supportive and safe environment.

The environment allowed the young part to go the distance, explore, and expand its vision of a happier self filled with joy, freedom, and creativity.

The younger part had to experience the vision to manifest its deepest desires—a big step for the parts to shift their story and transform their beliefs.

For the first time, I felt a profound relief when the uncertain young part felt safe to explore and go the distance.

Once the gatekeeper and the young part felt safe to explore further, another part unexpectedly came to the surface and revealed itself. Each part has different layers, each one revealing the hidden truth.

"I just wanted to keep you safe, hidden, and unseen."

People have asked me many times, "Why are you hiding?

Why stay behind a mic?" Why not share your wisdom with more people?

They've told me, This message is so important—it needs to reach millions.

They've said, an inspiration… you're a gift to the world... Why are you playing small? Why hide? Why not shine?

Now I understand why.

At first, this part resisted any form of visibility; it didn't want to be seen; being seen was scary. But as it started to change its belief, it felt safe, gradually transforming the fear, liberating the parts that held the fear of rejection and judgment. This was a crucial step in its pursuit of fulfilling its desires and releasing itself from limitations.

The fear of being seen is real. It's unconscious, and we might not even realize it—a part of our past wants to stay hidden. This part influences our choices, how we show up, and how we act.

Remember, what we resist is what we seek; it's our void. Time brings us what we focus on. This young part, unknown to me, wanted to stay hidden.

I can't count how many times I've felt this resistance. I'd chase my dreams and goals, not realizing this part was holding me back, saying, "Stop. You're going too far. It's scary. You're standing out. It's not safe. Step back." This pattern was so familiar. Have you ever experienced hitting an invisible wall?

I had hit an invisible barrier, a wall I couldn't climb, and I wondered why I couldn't break through. I had put all my energy and effort into this, yet I was still stuck with no progress.

It made me realize how much these parts influenced my life. I would only feel fulfilled if I found a way for them to change and grow. I now understand the profound impact of including these parts in my grand life vision. It's empowering for these parts when they transition, and their fears have transformed.

This experience shifted my perspective on these parts, revealing their layers, and I realized their impact on my life. I now understand. The fearful parts that held the fear believed it was safer to be invisible and hide than to be seen.

But to heal that fear, we need to establish safety for the parts to fulfill their desire. We seek what we resist and avoid. Being seen means our existence matters.

It validates and acknowledges the essence of who we are.

> *"I never thought anyone would notice me; I felt invisible. It's amazing that you see and appreciate me. You've shown me that you value and recognize something special in me."*

> *"You see me for who I am and appreciate that. Even though I've tried everything to keep you from standing out, you never gave up on me; you showed me that you value and accept me. I've been the one trying to hide your brightness, but now I see that your light isn't just bright—it's a force for change. The more I tried to hide it, the more it shone and lit up everything around it. Your brilliance has inspired me to step aside. I'm tired of trying to put out your light. You're like a sky full of stars, shining bright. Your impact on others is deep. Yet, here I am, still trying to dim your brilliance, but the more I try, the more you illuminate, and the more I realize I can't stop you."*

Once a safe connection was established, the parts continued sharing. It was in their own words, yet those words were very familiar to me: *"I felt as if I didn't matter; my existence was of no worth or value. I was invisible."*

"I was afraid of your stardom. Your dreams scared me, and even the idea of appearing on TV with Oprah was too much. I didn't want you to pursue your dreams; I was worried you would not be valued and would be rejected and forgotten. I found comfort in staying hidden; it was the safest thing to do. I kept you safe from the spotlight; it was safer to be invisible."

It went on:

"You have big dreams for your life, like making a TV show and writing books. But these goals scare me. They take you to new and unknown places, and I worry people won't value or appreciate your work. It feels safer to stay where we are; going to unfamiliar places is unsafe. I'm not comfortable going the distance."

The parts shared their fears and past experiences, feeling seen, heard, and safe in a space where they could speak freely. It's not about being invisible but about being valued and seen. Now, this part is experiencing what safety feels like.

The part continues: *"You brought me here, trusted me, and invited me to witness your vision. This means that you acknowledge my presence and appreciate me. I am not invisible to you because you see me. By trusting me with your vision, you believe I am capable and deserving of being part of it. This makes me feel valued and appreciated by you."*

The invisible parts feel seen, valued, and appreciated; they now believe their presence and existence mean something.

For this to work, safety must first be established.

The part acknowledges its limitations and expresses the following: *'I now see that I've played a part in making you feel small and unseen, dimming your light. I didn't want you to stand out and shine brightly. But I realize now that even when I was invisible, you still valued and appreciated me. You saw me for who I am and found worth in me."*

Part transitioning to a super-part.

"Who am I to prevent you from shining and sharing your light with the world? Who am I to hold you back from making a meaningful and valuable impact that could change many lives?"

"Who am I to stand in your way?"

At that moment, the parts understood why they acted as they did. I acknowledged their experience, saying, "I understand you better now." Then, I asked them,

Given what you know, how do you want to proceed?

Also, this happens as the part has gone through the safe passage, started transitioning, and is fully engaged in the vision we've created.

The parts response:

"I'm so happy here. It feels amazing and freeing to just be myself. This place makes me feel so comfortable being who I truly am. I absolutely love this space; it feels like home to me. It's where I belong. I'm rewriting my story. I've made the decision not to stay confined to my old narrative anymore. Through this transformation, I've become the best version of my story. I made the choice to be here."

The part rewrites its story and becomes a transformed part.

The parts' transformation process: *"I'm not here to hold you back anymore. I'm taking off the veil that's been hiding your potential. I'm removing it completely so you can shine brightly in the world. I'll lift you up with the same energy and strength I once used to keep you hidden. I'll raise you high so you can share your light and change lives."*

Before this process, I didn't even know these hidden parts existed.

But during this journey, I managed to turn those invisible parts into something powerful by working with them. Now, I see how crucial it is to recognize, validate, and appreciate all the different parts that defined and shaped my life.

Are you struggling to reach your goals and bring your dreams to life?

Ever wondered why your vision seems so far away?

Have you thought about how the parts you've been trying to get rid of might actually be essential for achieving your goals?

Have you ever considered how those parts you try to push away might feel?

Every time you ignore or dismiss them, you're hurting them. You're basically saying they don't matter.

Now, picture what happens when these parts go through this transformation. It's life-changing!

Each part has a role to play because each part serves a purpose.

To achieve your grand vision—whether it's finding success, love, or making a big impact—you need all these parts to work together. Each part is like a superpower, helping to bring your vision to life.

Once held confined with limitations, these parts now feel liberated and empowered. They can embrace their unique qualities and talents, showing their true potential. This is when you truly unleash your superpower.

You have an incredible ability to transform these parts. Your vision isn't just a far-off dream; it's something you can achieve and manifest. As you journey through this transformation, you'll learn to go the distance with no parts left behind. And you'll emerge inspired and empowered. You're incredibly powerful when your vision aligns with these super-parts.

Just imagine creating your dream vision with these superpowers! You'll be unstoppable. Nothing will be out of reach. Everything you need is already inside you; you can achieve anything and make your soul's vision a reality.

Moment of Reflection

CHAPTER FIFTEEN
Assigning Goals to Your Vision

Your Vision is assigned to you.

Don't rush into setting goals until your parts have transitioned, transformed, and gone through the breakthrough process. Otherwise, you'll keep running into roadblocks.

I'm not saying goal setting isn't important. Often, the way we set goals doesn't match what's going on inside us. This mismatch is why we keep facing obstacles that seem impossible to overcome. Alignment is key, but it's something that happens inside you. Your epic vision and the parts that believe in your vision need to be aligned.

Ever feel stuck, like you're hitting a wall you can't, see? It's not your fault. You're not alone.

Even though I did everything I could think of—setting goals, making vision boards, building good habits—I still struggled to progress. Despite spending time daily on my vision, listening to audio and video, and reading many books, I kept running into an invisible wall.

To make your vision real, these parts need to be in sync with it first.

When things don't line up, it can be frustrating trying to make your dreams happen. You end up spending a lot of time, energy, and money on endless programs.

I get it because I've been there too. It's okay to invest in programs that help us grow. Learning is necessary for our growth! But sometimes, we get so caught up in gathering information that we forget why we are doing it in the first place. We get stuck, hitting that invisible wall over and over.

It feels like a never-ending cycle. But remember, you're not alone, and there's a way out. Have you considered that the answers you are seeking might already be within you? Do you still feel stuck even with all the knowledge and wisdom you have gained?

Is your vision out of reach? It might be time to pause and reflect.

What if, instead of trying to break through an invisible wall, we find a way to go through it? How could that change our lives? And perhaps the most important question: Why haven't I figured out how to break through this invisible wall yet?

Even when your vision is clear, you may find something is blocking you from manifesting it.

I couldn't understand what prevented me from manifesting my epic vision, so I focused on finding a way through the invisible wall. What's in the way of my epic dream?

What's the purpose of the invisible wall?

You know you have what it takes to pursue your desired life. Yet, there's an invisible wall stopping you from manifesting your vision.

As I explored, I became more curious, which led me to discover the gap; I realized that there was a huge gap between setting goals and manifesting them.

You know you've got what it takes to make your dreams come true.

So, what's next? It's about finding a way through that invisible wall and understanding its secret.

Remember, you're the architect of your destiny. You can't fix what you can't see. So, to manifest your vision, you must get past the invisible wall. That's the focus as you start this journey: not breaking walls or eliminating beliefs but going the distance, leaving no parts behind.

Think about it: the actions you've taken so far have yet to produce the desired outcomes. Why not consider new possibilities? It's time to take a bold step, seize the moment, and rewrite your incredible story, turning your dream into a reality.

I went through a transformational process. It was a holistic approach that created change with each part. The parts helped me rewrite my story, a new chapter in my life going the distance, leaving no parts behind.

Before you set goals, you need to imagine and bring to life your big vision, getting all your parts in line with it. This process helps you let go of any limits and turn them into superpowers. Then, your goals become clearer because you're coming from a place of abundance.You've gone through the wall because there's no more pushback. The parts that once resisted, like self-doubt or fear, have changed and are now on board with your vision.

This change is crucial and a big part of making your vision real. You start a breakthrough process when you change and align your habits and beliefs with your vision. You approach your goals from a place of abundance.

The parts that were once scared of change have transformed into superpowers. Once the threat of uncertainty and fear is gone, the parts will no longer resist change and will be aligned with the vision. Just imagine the transformative difference in your life once these parts are empowered. Everything gets rewired, and beliefs and habits are aligned with your vision. Can you imagine the impact on your daily life and the significant steps you'll take toward manifesting your goals and vision? The parts are all on the same page as your vision now.

Empowered Parts

When creating your grand vision, you might think you can do it alone. But every part is a co-author and co-creator of your vision. It's about bringing all these parts together and recognizing that each has a role and unique abilities. When you empower each part to transform, you're no longer limited and begin to experience the abundance.

You have something valuable to give and a story worth sharing. You have meaningful contributions to make. When you approach your vision with certainty, as if it's already manifested, this process allows you to see which parts are no longer serving the growth of your vision. These parts are unaware of their superpower, and you can help them reconnect to their unique abilities.

Each part creates its vision and has goals it wants to achieve. To succeed, you need to make sure no part is left behind. Every part must support and align with your vision. Only then will you be able to manifest the life you desire.

This is the missing piece. The parts are not aligned with your vision and, therefore, cannot support your growth. That's why you keep facing the same obstacles. These parts haven't been included in your vision. You need to bring them on board. They must feel safe and certain of your vision. Only then will they go the distance and empower you to manifest your epic vision.

Why? Because the parts will have experienced the vision as already manifested and will align with your goals with clarity and certainty.

The message is clear: Don't set goals until you've gone through this process. Otherwise, you'll keep running into the same invisible wall.

Moment of Reflection

CHAPTER SIXTEEN
Show Me the Vision

Extending the invitation to the parts.

Here is what the conversation with the parts would look like:
I completely understand the hesitation and resistance. The idea of manifesting a grand vision can be daunting and uncertain. Taking risks and stepping into the unknown can be uncomfortable and scary.

It's normal to feel uneasy. I get it. Going the distance may seem unsafe and uncertain, making you feel unsure about entering unknown territory. I am here to support you and help you realize our shared vision.

I invite you to see the vision I see for you and us.

Imagine inviting these fearful parts that fear the unknown and uncertainty and saying to them, *come along; I want to show you the vision.*

Manifesting our vision can be challenging when we fear uncertainty or the unknown. However, a powerful technique can help us overcome these challenges.

Imagine inviting those fearful parts to join you and see your vision as if it has already happened. By doing this, you show these parts what life looks like when you've achieved your goals. You show them that the vision is not in the future but already exists in the present moment. This technique can help you temporarily set aside fear and overcome any obstacles.

Anytime you find yourself stuck, remember to invite the fearful parts and show them the vision.

The part is curious now: Why? The part only knows the past. It hasn't seen the vision yet. It's scared of the unknown. "Come with me; I'm here with you every step of the way. I want to show you the vision I have designed, created, and manifested, and I am committed to guiding you towards it."

You are inviting the fearful parts of uncertainty, like the fear of the unknown, the fear of failure, or any other fear that holds you back. You can work with this for now. However, imagine the power you have when you can use the same process without fear, beliefs, or limitations. The possibilities are endless, and you are in control.

In this process, you are not eliminating any of these parts; you are inviting them to experience the vision as already manifested. This is crucial for creating a safe passage for these parts to transition and transform. They need to know there are no threats to their safety. So, you must clarify your vision and show these parts of the vision as already manifested. By doing this, you create a safe experience for these parts.

Once these parts experience the manifested vision, the fear of the unknown and uncertainty is no longer a threat. These parts see the vision as real and feel safe for the first time. The release for these parts will be like this: it's done and complete; there's nothing to worry about and nothing to protect.

It's a revolutionary way of being. Now, the fearful part of the unknown sees what you see. Before, these parts didn't have the complete picture of your vision. Extend a special invitation to co-design your epic vision.

As a token of gratitude, the most honourable thing to do when rewriting your story is to invite these parts to help co-design your epic vision. Personalizing the conversation creates a sense of safety.

Here's what to say:

I want us to rewrite our story. Each part of you is welcome and invited to help rewrite our story.

Inviting the fear of the unknown and uncertainty to experience the vision as already manifested can be truly transformative. The most epic moment is when these parts realize the peace and tranquility of being in a safe space, no longer bound by uncertainty or the unknown.

Why?

It's crucial to follow through with this process and continue to believe the vision is already complete and manifested.

It's complete; it's already manifested. You have manifested your vision. There's nothing to fear.

Remember, these parts are still holding on to the past and need to feel safe and secure to move forward.

The key is to remove the threat that holds them back, which can only happen when these parts experience the vision as complete and manifested. This will allow these parts to experience a safe passage and realize there is nothing to fear. Once this happens, you'll notice a positive shift in your body—these parts will communicate with you, and you'll feel a sense of ease and relief.

Parts Transforming and Redefining their Story.

The moment the fearful part realizes there is no threat to its safety, it feels safe and understands there's no reason to be afraid. Fear subsides, and it begins to relax and enjoy the freedom of not worrying.

While experiencing the manifestation of the vision, the hidden layer of fear resurfaces, a fear deeply rooted in memory; it wasn't just fear of the unknown but much more profound.

These fearful parts now feel comfortable and safe enough to share even more. You find it wasn't about the unknown or uncertainty; it was more profound. By acknowledging and validating these fears, they gradually release their hold on you, and you discover a newfound sense of freedom and peace.

How I revolutionized and transformed the parts.

The parts I'm very familiar with and have worked with have held onto the fear of the unknown and uncertainty. When these parts finally experienced the vision as real, there was an immediate sigh of relief, a comforting embrace of the known. That's when the other layers of these parts opened and started sharing.

Not long after, I recognized the rejected and abandoned parts also held fear. These parts opened even more, revealing their pain and vulnerability.

Here's the revelation I received from these parts, and I want to honour them as they communicated with me.

I'm using the parts' words directed to me: *"Our fear is when you create your vision and go to the distance; it scares us; it's not the unknown we fear most. We are worried that you will abandon us. Being left alone makes us feel unworthy and no longer needed. We don't want to be left alone; it will make us sad."*

Here's what I learned from the experience. When you pursue your goals and vision, fear arises. But this fear isn't about the unknown but being left behind. We all want to feel like we belong and matter, and the thought of being abandoned is scary.

Feeling sad about being alone is normal, but my role was to remind them they are valued and appreciated, that they are a vital part of my life, and that they matter.

Creating a safe space is crucial in our journey of self-exploration and healing. It allows these parts to open and share their deepest fears. The "gatekeeper" is often our first line of defense, and it needs immediate attention. The fear of the unknown and uncertainty act as gatekeepers. Once these parts feel safe, other layers reveal themselves.

When the parts feel safe and trust your vision, they feel secure enough to trust you. When these parts trust you, they reveal their source of pain and fear.

Beneath that fear. it says:

> *"It wasn't the uncertainty of the unknown in pursuing the vision that held me back. The truth is, I feared you would leave me behind, that you didn't include me in this journey, that you would forget about me, that you would reject me."*

The parts revealed their deepest fears when they felt safe and secure and shared their fear of being left alone.

During the experience, I realized it wasn't the uncertainty of the unknown that held me back from achieving my vision. It was the fear of being left behind; the part that felt abandoned and rejected was the fear of being alone again. The painful emotion of sadness was what the gatekeepers worked hard to protect me from the pain of sadness and loneliness by focusing on the surface-level fear of the unknown.

When these parts resurfaced, it was a vulnerable moment. I recognized them; they were familiar, stemming from my childhood, the fear of being left alone. Establishing safety and sharing the vision with the parts creates certainty for them. The message is clear: going the distance means no parts are left behind. These parts are certain they are coming along, and you are not abandoning or rejecting them.

Significantly, their energy shifts once these parts express the hidden fears beneath the surface.

These parts feel seen, heard, and valued for the first time. They feel worthy enough to be part of our vision and journey. It isn't just a process; it's a journey, they are a part of it.

This creates a sense of wholeness and completeness, which is crucial for our emotional and mental well-being. Remembering to include and transform all parts of ourselves is vital to achieving our vision and living a fulfilling, meaningful life.

Have you considered working with fear instead of trying to get rid of it? No matter how hard you try, fear can't be destroyed or eliminated. Instead, focus on evolving and transforming the fear parts. When fear is transformed into something greater, it can become a superpower within you. So, embrace fears and use them to manifest your vision.

Parts Transitioning and Aligning with Your Vision.

Part two of the process

When parts realize they are stuck in the past but see a vision of what's possible, they understand their limits and potential. As they return to their true selves, they evolve, choose their path forward, and transform their beliefs to become their best selves. You don't force the transformation; you support it. Once the parts have transformed, they will align with your vision.

This process can change how you approach these parts. It guides you to see them with openness, compassion, understanding, and curiosity. It's not about eliminating limiting beliefs, which you may have tried and found ineffective. It's about a revolutionary, transformative approach that acknowledges and validates these parts and past efforts while offering a new path for growth and transformation.

Instead, empower these parts to rewrite their own story. This means acknowledging their presence, understanding their origin, and reframing them positively. That's the way forward to your vision— not by eliminating, getting rid of, or overcoming them. Empowering these parts is not about eliminating or overcoming them.

When these parts redefine their beliefs and embrace their true purpose, which is abundant and supportive, they stop holding you back.

When these parts return to their original state, it's like a rebirth of their purpose.

The real power of this process is its ability to transform our beliefs. As you go on this journey, your beliefs evolve into powerful forces that align perfectly with your vision, empowering you to take control of your life. Imagine moving forward with supercharged beliefs. Every step toward your vision is boosted by these powerful beliefs.

It's a rebirth of your inner strengths, which is truly empowering. Picture the life you can create when your beliefs align with your vision. It's a life of abundance, success, and fulfillment, one that you have the power to attract and create.

Instead of trying to eliminate these parts, it's much more powerful to help them redefine and transform their role and purpose. To manifest your vision, you need to bring all these parts along the journey, letting each of them experience what achieving a great vision feels and looks like.

It's not just about bringing these parts along on your vision. It's about freeing them from their limitations, as they are parts of the past, stuck in old patterns.

You want to help these parts see what freedom looks like. Ultimately, these parts want to be free from the past so they can also experience their highest potential.

Once these parts are freed from the past and aligned with your vision, something magical happens: the past no longer takes up space, on the following chapter explore why it's important to create passage for your vision to receive abundance.

Moment of Reflection

CHAPTER SEVENTEEN
Creating a Safe Passage

You will manifest your vision when these parts have transformed into their best selves.

What comes after the magical moment of transitioning these parts? Once these parts are freed from the past and aligned with your vision, something magical happens: the past no longer takes up space.

The next step is to create space for your vision.

The past occupies this space; you must create room to hold your vision. By freeing these parts and letting them transition, you create the space to receive the abundance—room for your evolved self, room for these parts to reach their highest potential, and room to receive and hold your epic vision. To go the distance and manifest your grand vision, you must create the room for it.

Just imagine: If your vision occupies this space, what potential for personal growth and transformation could you unlock?

Self-exploration exercise

When exploring your personal experiences, it's important to focus on one part at a time.

1. By working through one part of your life that's currently present, you can start to peel back the layers and understand its impact on you.

2. Once you've created a safe space for this part to evolve and transition, you can invite other parts to join the journey. Remember, taking things one step at a time can make a big difference in your overall growth and development.

My communication process with the parts

To fully understand and integrate all parts, I invited each part, both conscious and unconscious. I knew there might be parts I wasn't aware of, so I invited them all. By doing this, I aimed to better understand the parts and myself and achieve greater harmony.

This is how I approached them:

I want to extend a special invitation to all of you to experience our epic vision. Come and see what we have achieved. Now that you have seen the vision and know with certainty that it is possible and real, what fear still lies beneath the uncertainty or unknown?"

Then the parts replied: "*The uncertainty that came with the fear was overwhelming, making me sad. It wasn't just about not knowing where you were going but also about not wanting you to leave without me. The fear of being left behind and forgotten was real, making me feel unsafe and unimportant. I worry that you may no longer need me or see any value in me, which makes me sad.*"

That was the initial response. The uncertain parts went through the safety passage while immersed in the vision. There was no fear because the parts felt safe while experiencing the vision. I spoke to these parts as if they had already manifested the vision, creating a sense of safety.

Here's my dialogue with the parts that experienced the vision for the first time:

"I feel safe enough to express myself here."

I understand, I responded. I get it, and I understand why you feel that way. How do you feel when you are here?

The parts respond with:

"I feel loved. It's exciting to be here."

I then respond with:

Then this is your home. Imagine waking up here every morning. Would you be open to it?

Part responds:

"Yes, I'm open to it."

Then I say:

Go for it.

I communicated and created a safe space for the parts, allowing them to recognize and experience the vision.

The parts' response:

"I get to see and experience this vision. I get to be here. Do I get to experience this with you?"

Yes.

"So, you're not leaving me behind. You're not going to abandon me?"

No, you're coming with me.

"I am coming with you."

The part felt immensely empowered and made a commitment. It promised to use the same energy and focus that once held back to now uplift and elevate.

The part added:

'This is what you're manifesting for me and the rest of us. I want to be present every morning, to wake up to this new version of me."

Following this experience, I felt a deep sense of calm and inner peace all day. I noticed the part was emersed in peace and calm; I felt my body expand as if a space had opened within me. Even more impressive was the chatter in my mind disappeared; it was pure, uninterrupted peace. The experience taught me the value of embracing all parts and not leaving any behind. Isn't it incredible when we fully experience all aspects of our being?

When you envision your life's grand design, it's crucial to include all parts, even the ones you might consider less desirable. Embracing these parts, rather than avoiding or rejecting them, is key to manifesting your vision and taking full control of your life's story.

Your highest version, where you are at your best and most fulfilled, will manifest when these parts have transformed into their best selves. It's not just about reaching a peak but consistently striving for growth and fulfillment. Once these parts experience transformation, it will feel like this.

"I am safe. It's a great place to be. I am at peace and secure and no longer need to worry. I feel a deep sense of calm and contentment."

When these parts' highest versions are transformed, your highest version will show up.

Once these parts experience the process, they'll feel safe and at peace.

They feel safe; it's a safe place. They no longer need to worry; They can just be.

When you guide these parts to experience the vision, you lead them to a place of relief and freedom where they can let go of their worries, fears, and limitations. This is when you create a safe space for them to release their burdens and transform into what they desire.

It's crucial for these parts to trust you and feel safe enough to open up and share. This is key to realizing your vision. Your vision should clearly state: No parts left behind.

By going the distance, manifesting your vision, and ensuring no parts are left behind, you achieve personal growth and align with all parts of your being. This unity brings purpose and direction to your journey.

Personal transformation and manifesting your vision involve integrating these parts and seeing the vision as already real. This step is crucial and can greatly accelerate your personal transformation.

It's important for the parts to fully immerse themselves in the vision with certainty and feel the freedom from fear. As they transform, they evolve. Remember, it's not about assigning roles but about empowering them to define their own roles once they have overcome their fears.

Now, these parts are free from fear. The space that fear once occupied is now open and expansive, and you can feel it in your body—an immediate expansion. This expansion isn't just a physical sensation but a symbol of the vast potential and possibilities that come with the transformation process.

Moment of Reflection

CHAPTER EIGHTEEN
Making Room to Receive Abundance

This approach brings your epic vision to life.

Remember, for abundance to flow into your life, you must first make room for it. Where will the abundance flow if you don't have room to receive it? This simple understanding can revolutionize and transform your life.

Creating space for abundance is crucial to manifesting what you desire. Your internal space must be clear and open to receive it. This means recognizing the need to make room within yourself to welcome abundance.

When these parts transition and transform their roles, they become superpowers. They leave the space they once occupied and move into the vision you have created, creating more room. This space becomes open and expansive.

As you transform these parts, they transition with the vision and become your superpowers. In the process, they no longer occupy the space, allowing abundance to flow in.

You will feel your energy shifting, an inner expansion flowing with abundance. This will ignite new desires and aspirations, and you will notice a change in how you show up. Work with the parts to receive and manifest the abundance in your life.

Empower yourself by creating space for abundance to flow. This transformative process allows your epic vision to manifest, aligning you with the frequency of your desired vision.

Transforming fear is not just part of the process; it's necessary. By transitioning fear with your vision and evolving, you clear space to receive the abundance of your vision.

You need to clear a path for the vision to flow and manifest. Make room to receive abundance and manifest your vision. When you align with all parts of your epic vision, there's no resistance. You become one with the parts. You're not battling or opposing each other; instead, you're moving forward together, with no parts left behind and fully aligned with your vision.

Creating Space for Manifestation

You need space to manifest your vision and receive abundance in your life. You can't receive abundance if there's no room for it. You need to recognize this and create space within yourself.

This process happens holistically and authentically. When a part transitions and takes on a new role, it embodies different energy and no longer occupies the same space; it moves to a new space. By doing this, the part clears the space it once held, making it available. As the part transforms, you feel a sense of expansion within. Suddenly, you feel the energy opening, the depth of the space, and the serenity and expansion within.

By clearing the space, you create room to receive the abundance you want to attract and manifest.

Remember, until now, you didn't have the space to receive it because these parts occupied it. These parts were there for reasons you understand well. You must go through the process. Now that you know how to manifest what you desire, you must create the space to receive it.

For instance, to manifest a loving relationship, ask yourself what is occupying the space. Is there room to receive a loving relationship? Have you cleared the space to receive love? If not, it's time to look within, include all parts, and follow the process. These parts must be part of your vision, including a loving relationship.

What if pain and heartbreak occupy the space?

Do you have space to receive love? Would you recognize love when pain is in the way? If not, then it's time to clear that space and make room for what you desire. Go the distance with no parts left behind; you will be amazed by what comes through for you.

Each part knows your innermost desires and wants.

Each part knows what it needs. Remember, these parts know you very well. Deep inside, they know your soul's desires. These parts have protected your innermost wants and desires.

With that understanding, the role of these parts is to bring your innermost desires to your attention. These parts will awaken and ignite the fire of your soul's desires. They will uplift you, wake you up, and remind you of what you truly desire.

Automatically, you find yourself in a flow. These parts are no longer working against you; they're working with you, co-creating and rewriting your story. They know when it's time to clear out of the space.

You have your vision, and so do these parts. These parts represent different aspects of your personality, experiences, and desires. They have unique desires and aspirations based on their past experiences.

The previous function of these parts was not to prevent you from manifesting your vision. You have the power to align your visions and manifest your dreams by creating a shared vision with these parts.

When these parts experience the manifestation of the vision, they will communicate it to you. They will say, "We've seen the vision you manifested. You valued us and brought us along. We've seen what's possible. We are certain it is possible to manifest your vision. We're in the middle of it." This certainty is what the parts need to experience.

This is the moment these parts transition from the space they occupied and move to a new space, clearing the space they once held.

Remember that you can design your life exactly how you want it to be. My invitation is to leave no parts behind as you pursue your grand vision. By working towards a shared vision and making space for the abundance your soul desires, you can create the life of your dreams.

Moment of Reflection

CHAPTER NINETEEN
Time Revelations

Time delivers what you spend time on.

In this chapter, I want to introduce you to new concepts on time. I'm not talking about time management because you've learned that already. I've taken so many time management programs and courses. Through the breakthrough process, I discovered new insights about time. I'll share my understanding of time and how I choose to use it.

I was doing some inner work, visualizing my vision as already manifested, and began journaling the experience shortly after meditating.

I wrote these words in my journal:

I am amazed at how quickly I can bring my vision to life. Manifesting my desires has become effortless and abundant, allowing me to achieve my goals with ease and grace.

I recently realized that time is not separate from me or a destination to reach. Instead, I flow and exist with time. Time is always present. Time always shows up and delivers what I spend it on.

That was a massive shift for me. It hit me: time delivers what I spend time on.

I realized that spending time on irrelevant things leads to irrelevant results. However, focusing on my aspirations time will deliver outcomes that align with my vision.

I discovered the key to unlocking time to manifest my epic vision:

If time isn't separate from me, then I can bring it closer. Time is here, right now. It flows with me, and I flow with it. We're not separate from each other.

I recognize that time delivers what I spend it on; it delivers what I desire because I spend my time creating my epic vision.

This wasn't just a breakthrough but a profound "Ah-ha" moment that changed my life.

Realizing that time can bring me what I focus on, I started to amplify my desire to achieve my epic vision.

Here's my truth: time has delivered my vision of sharing my life lessons with you, and my desire has become a reality. It's happening as you read this book. I want to acknowledge your dedication and engagement in this journey, and exploring new possibilities.

Reflecting on the chapters you've read; we can assume you've made significant progress. Let's quickly review where you are now:

1. You have defined the vision you want to achieve.

2. You are fully committed, leaving no parts behind.

3. Every part of you aligns with your big vision.

4. You have connected with your highest self.

5. You have made space to welcome the abundance your soul desires. Now, what's next?

You need to boost and speed up your vision by having time on your side. Work with time to achieve your epic vision faster, aligning it with the right frequency to manifest your dreams.

Treat time as your ally, not an obstacle. You and time are connected, not separate. Your dreams aren't distant but visions waiting to align with time. This is the key to unlocking your potential. Time is a powerful partner that can help you achieve your desires.

Invest your time in manifesting your vision, and time will respond by delivering it. The more time you dedicate to your vision, the sooner you'll reach your goals and realize your grand dreams.

Time delivers to you what you spend it on.

When it comes to changing and improving your life, spend time creating the space for these changes to happen. If you avoid this, time will deliver what you neglect. The result matches the time you invest.

Time will deliver result proportional to the time and energy we put into it.

Why?

These parts chose to change with time. Time is part of the process and helps these parts transition. You spent time with these parts, and they transformed their way of being.

Time also plays a role in delivering the vision as already manifested, allowing the parts to experience it. Time is always present and essential in manifesting your vision. Remember, time delivers your vision as already manifested.

Time affects the transformation process. When parts choose to change, time becomes crucial in their transition. Time is vital in delivering the already manifested vision and is always present in making our dreams come true.

Time shows up in the present moment. It's important to use time when these parts are transitioning. They can only transform when they are in the present, experiencing the future.

Time is key in the transformation process, and it's necessary to be present to experience your vision. Using time when parts are transitioning helps them move from the past into the present.

Breakthrough I discovered with time.

We have learned that to succeed, we need an accountability partner. This process might work for some and not for others. But here's the catch: how can one person be responsible and accountable for another's results? When it comes to the things that matter to you, you need to be accountable for that.

I've realized that time is the best accountability partner. You partner with time whenever you engage in any activity, and time is always on your side.

Here's another eye-opener: time is not just a ticking clock or a resource; it's your unwavering accountability partner. No one will hold you accountable more than time. It records how you spend it, showing your priorities and actions. Time always delivers based on what you invest in it. No one else can match the steadfastness and reliability of time in this role.

Time is your ultimate accountability partner. It will deliver what you spend time on and hold you accountable.

So, instead of trying to manage time, I invite you to develop a relationship with it. When you do this and hold yourself accountable for how you spend your time, you'll find an abundance of time on your side.

Here's yet another revelation with time.

Communicate your epic vision with time.

Time is not just a passive observer in your journey; it's a powerful ally waiting to be engaged. By sharing your vision and the timeline you want to achieve it, you are not just informing time but empowering it to deliver your vision.

Achieving your long-term goals is a journey closely linked with time. Understand that you and time are inseparable. Time is a constant companion, always there for you. Recognizing this and knowing that time is always by your side makes it clear that sharing your grand vision with time is essential.

You have done well in communicating your vision and making room to receive its abundance. You also need time, as it is part of your journey. Time is not separate from you. It's here now, always present. Time delivers based on what you spend it on.

Time will not only hold you accountable but will deliver results. Time is also accountable to you and will give you exactly what you invest your time in. Time speaks to you and says, "I'm your accountability partner, and I will deliver what you spend your time on. If you spend time on things of no value, then that's what I will deliver."

The impact of time comes when you approach it as your highest self. Being clear about your vision and fully committed means you show up as your highest self. You will spend time being that version and taking actions aligned with your vision and highest self.

Time delivers exactly what you envision. Therefore, you need to develop a relationship with time. Treat time as if it is always on your side. Time always shows up for you.

Time Revelation and Breakthrough

You manifest what you spend time on.

The outcomes and results in your life are closely tied to how you use time. Reflect on what you spend your time on and ensure it aligns with your goals and dreams. Time flows through your life and everything you do. It's not a destination or something to manage but a constant companion that needs your attention and focus. Time always moves forward, but it's up to you to decide how you engage with it.

Do you invest your time in things that matter to you?

Do you prioritize your time to serve your purpose?

Ask yourself these questions to ensure you create a fulfilling life with time. Remember, time delivers what you spend it on. Time is your most valuable accountability partner.

What are you co-creating with time?

Are you aware of the power of co-creating with time?

Remember that you and time coexist and co-create your reality. This understanding can transform your life. Time is not your enemy; it's your ally in achieving your goals and dreams. Time is abundant and ever-flowing, always available to you. It doesn't punish you but holds you accountable for how you use it. It is a kind and generous force that gives you what you spend your time on.

Time never takes away from you. It is always providing and never stops giving.

How you spend your time determines the life you create; every moment is an opportunity to co-create your reality with time.

So, what are you co-creating with time?

My question to you now is: How are you choosing to invest your time?

If you invest your time in activities that create chaos, be prepared for time to reflect that chaos back to you.

If you spend your time complaining, time delivers proof of what you are complaining about.

Time, like a patient friend, is always by your side, waiting for you to make the most of it. It never gives back the hours you've spent, but it does hold you accountable for how you've used them. In this way, time is forgiving.

Here's a message from time.

I've noticed that when you set goals for your vision, you try so hard to control and manage time. Remember, I am always on your side; your vision should include me, not exclude me.

Think of me as a powerful tool, whispering, I am at your service, ready to be shaped by your choices. How you use me is what I'll manifest for you. Time, a steadfast companion, assures you, I'm always here, ready for you. You have me; use me as you see fit. Just remember, I'll faithfully reflect what you invest in me.

Imagine time as a personal guide, saying to you, I am here for you; however you choose to use me, that's what I'll deliver to you.

We often feel like we need more time because we haven't built a relationship with it and approach it with a mindset of scarcity rather than abundance.

However, we can change how we see time by letting go of our attachment to it and expressing gratitude. I have done this by appreciating and communicating my gratitude for the time I have.

Dear Time, I want to express my deep gratitude for all you have done for me. Your constant presence has allowed me to live, learn, and grow, shaping my very being. Even when I haven't used you wisely, you have always shown up and provided me with ample opportunities for growth and self-improvement. Your generosity and consistency are truly remarkable.

Thank you for being such an important part of my life. You have been a great gift to me, a generous and reliable force. I am truly grateful for your constant presence and generosity. Thank you for being such a vital part of my life.

I encourage you to build a relationship with time—a partnership that helps you achieve your desires. By dedicating time to your goals and aspirations, you align your actions with what you want time to deliver. This approach shapes your journey and allows you to engage in activities that reflect your deepest dreams. In doing so, you actively participate in its flow, co-creating and shaping your experiences and outcomes with time.

When you have a relationship with time, it's also about sharing your deepest desires and aspirations with it. You're telling time that you're creating a vision and need its cooperation, making it feel understood and valued.

When you surrender to time, you acknowledge its constant presence and importance. You understand that time is a vital part of the creation process. Time, in turn, assures you, "I've always been here, ready. I'm waiting for you to give me directions and tell me what you want me to deliver."

If you spend time doing nothing, time will deliver exactly that—nothing. Time, a generous gift, never takes away what you haven't used or adds what you haven't used.

How can you manage time? It's impossible. There's no need to squeeze out time. Let it flow abundantly. Letting go means not obsessing over every minute but focusing on your tasks and allowing time to progress naturally. Time is available to you when you stop trying to control it.

Remember, you have the power to align your vision with time. Time is not separate from you or a distant entity but a tool to shape your journey.

Going the distance with no parts left behind requires developing a relationship with time and working in partnership with it.

Creating a vision for your future is not just a task; it's an exciting journey. Your vision might feel big or far away, but it's important to remember that your vision coexists with time. You have the power to make it a reality. Your vision is not separate from time but a part of it.

To achieve your goals, it is essential to build a positive relationship with time and work with it. With dedication and a clear vision, time will help you manifest your dreams with ease and speed. Your vision is coming to life sooner than expected because time is on your side. You flow with time. You are in harmony with time, having developed a strong relationship with it.

Now, I want to share my recent experiences with time:

For the past year, I've been captivated by the idea of going on a safari in Tanzania. It's a dream I've nurtured and a desire that has grown daily. The thought of setting foot in Africa has been a constant vision that fuels my daily thoughts.

One day, while working on my computer and thinking about the safari, I briefly closed my eyes to visualize what I wanted to manifest. When I opened my eyes, I didn't realize the computer screen had gone to sleep. The first thing I saw on the screen amazed me.

It was a picture of a lion, the animal I had visualized during my meditation. I quickly grabbed my phone and took a photo, capturing the moment on January 1st, just before one in the afternoon. The scene on the screen looked like it was straight out of a nature documentary.

The image showed stunning scenery: majestic mountains with peaks piercing the sky, a lush green landscape, and a serene lakeside filled with birds and flamingos. I was especially drawn to the black and white zebras, their stripes standing out against the green grass. And, of course, the king of the jungle, the lion, added another layer of natural beauty to the picture. The top of the screen held the biggest surprise.

It was a sight that seemed to defy reality.

"Two worlds coexist harmoniously in what many consider the most beautiful place on earth, Tanzania, also known as the Eden of Africa."

Time will deliver what you spend time on. When we talk about manifesting our vision, time plays a crucial role in delivering it. Time can accelerate the process and bring our vision to life. What we spend our time thinking about tends to manifest in our lives.

Time will deliver the outcomes that match what we focus our time and energy on.

Therefore, it's essential to ensure we spend our time on the things that truly matter to us. By doing so, we can create the life we envision. I firmly believe in this concept because I have experienced it myself. By using time and focusing my energy on my vision, time delivered the image of the vision faster than I expected.

What do you spend your time on? What desire do you envision for time to deliver?

What you think about, time will deliver; what you focus on will manifest. The power of your thoughts and beliefs is immense. Your perception of time directly impacts your reality. Your thoughts and feelings can inspire you to manifest your desires. Sometimes, the best inspiration comes from the world around you.

It can be a message from a vision, an image on a computer screen, or a moment of contemplation. Even the challenges, disappointments, and heartbreaks you face in life can be sources of inspiration if you view them differently. Remember, every moment has the potential to inspire you to take a step forward.

Your higher version working with time.

I embrace curiosity when I'm in chaos. Every experience, no matter how wild, has a message. By facing each situation with an open mind and a desire to learn, I turn even the most challenging times into chances for personal growth and self-discovery.

Here's a practice you can try: First, take a deep breath and stay calm. This can help clear your mind and focus on what's happening. Then, ask yourself a few questions: What can I learn from this? What is this situation trying to teach me? What can I do differently next time? Facing chaos with curiosity and a willingness to learn can help you handle tough situations better and understand yourself and the world around you more deeply.

I am curious; What are you trying to tell me? What are you trying to teach me? What are you saying that I'm not hearing? What do I need to know that I haven't found out yet? Guide me on my journey. These reflections come from a place of curiosity that inspires growth, transformation, and healing.

Another incredible revelation—asking your higher version to step up.

As you go the distance, there will be a time when you need to call on the highest version to step in. Doing this sends a strong message to your higher self, showing you're ready to receive wisdom and guidance.

You are saying to your higher self: I need you. I've come to the peak of my journey, and I realize that what I know isn't enough to get the results I want.

One powerful technique is to be curious and ask questions, such as 'What is the next step in my personal growth journey?' or 'How can I overcome this challenge?'

This creates an opening for your higher self to step up and guide you.

The message you are sending to your higher self is simple: I am ready; I need you!

Have you ever wondered what happens when you ask, "Why is this happening to me? Is this it?"

You might not realize it, but you're not just asking questions; you are opening the door for change and growth.

It's easy to blame and judge ourselves when things don't go as planned. But remember self-criticism doesn't help us. The key to a breakthrough is to change our perspective and approach things from our highest self with kindness. Doing this enables us to handle challenges better and create a more fulfilling life.

Instead of focusing on what's not working, we should listen to our highest self's call to us. When we hear and understand this inner voice, it can guide us to a more fulfilling life.

By facing your experiences with curiosity and being present, you allow time to bring what you focus on. It's a great chance to spend some time alone with your thoughts and let time surprise you with what it has in store.

When you step out of the present moment, you attract a different kind of energy, and time responds to that. So, stay present and be open to the possibilities that time offers.

When you use your inner power and work with time, you ask powerful and meaningful questions that can lead to growth.

When you pay attention to the messages and listen to the inspiration around you, you create a space for your higher self to step in and take charge. To grow, you need to actively seek new information.

Follow the process:

1. To grow and evolve, it's important to know when you've reached your limit with what you know and can do.

2. Instead of feeling stuck or discouraged, see this as a chance to invite your higher self to guide you to your next level of growth.

3. Letting go of control and trusting the journey can help you reach your full potential and become your highest self. Trust the process and believe in your ability to grow and change.

When I feel I've reached my current limit, I know it's time for a deeper part of me, my 'higher self,' to step in. This higher self isn't some distant, unreachable goal but a part of me that's already here, ready to guide me toward my full potential. I understand the importance of knowing when I've reached my limits and let my higher self take over. I invite you to approach your higher self with the same understanding.

Your higher self is not a distant ideal but a reality that has already gone through many experiences and gained deep wisdom. It has valuable information that you don't have right now. Trusting your higher self's guidance is essential, especially when you feel you've reached your limits. By recognizing your higher self's presence and willingness to help, you open yourself up to new possibilities and growth.

Think of your higher self as a wiser, more experienced version of you that has already dealt with your current challenges. Remember that your higher self has overcome the challenges you face now. The one reading this knows there was a past higher self that got you to where you are now. Recognize and honour the many higher selves that have guided you this far.

When I need direction, I often turn to my highest self. I trust and believe in this wiser, more knowledgeable part of me and ask for guidance. This higher self already exists within me, holding insights and wisdom that I may not always see. By surrendering to this higher self, I feel empowered to move forward with clarity and purpose.

Now, think about your relationship with time. You've invited time into this conversation, and everything aligns to help you achieve your vision.

As you continue your journey, your 'highest self ', the version of you that is aligned with your true potential and values, continues to unfold.

If you knew your 'highest self ', the most authentic and fulfilled version of you, was already here, how would your life be different? I am confident that our highest self already exists. As you read this now, your highest self is not a distant concept but already present. You and I can access our highest selves right now. The one sharing this with you now is my highest self. I am excited to see the revealing of my highest self and yours.

How did I come to believe that our highest self exists? Our highest self is not a distant dream; it's already within us. The version we want to be is ready to step up. The current version of us must step aside for our highest self to take over. The version of us from the past, with all its experiences and lessons, doesn't disappear. It steps aside, making room for the highest self to help write the next chapter of our lives. The version we aspire to be is already within us.

This process of 'stepping aside' means acknowledging and learning from our past but not letting it define our future.

My current self is smart and wise, knowing when to step aside and let my next highest self take charge. I recognize that my higher self has knowledge, wisdom, and solutions to problems I haven't yet thought of. My higher self keeps surprising me with her abilities, and I learn from her while sharing my own wisdom with her.

Time is always with you on your journey to your highest potential. As you move forward, time helps you become your best self. Even if you haven't noticed it yet, looking back, you'll see that time has always brought out your highest self.

Think back to five years ago. Could you have imagined being where you are now? Yet, the version of yourself today already existed. From this point on, understand that your highest self is already here. The question is whether you will wait passively for months or years to see it or actively work with time to see your highest self now.

I have developed a close relationship with time. It's not just about seconds, minutes, and hours for me. Time is a companion, a partner in my personal growth journey. I have shared my vision and goals with time, expressing what I desire to manifest. I trust that time, as my loyal companion, will deliver what I desire. Time is not just part of my story; we work together, creating meaningful moments.

As I keep growing with time, each moment is a step in my personal growth and creating the life I want. I keep learning and gaining wisdom from my experiences; my story keeps evolving and shaping my journey.

I invite you to think about how you plan to use your time. Remember that the things you spend time on can help you achieve your goals. If there's something you want to accomplish, dedicate your time to it and be amazed at what time can deliver.

As you continue to grow and evolve, you may rediscover yourself. Even when you think you've reached your full potential, there may be layers to unearth. So, take time to explore and connect with your inner self, and you may be surprised at the hidden gems you find within.

Now that you have discovered these hidden gems, found the safe path through the invisible barriers, and developed a relationship with time, you have empowered yourself to change, transform, and reach your highest self. You know for certain that your desired vision exists, and you have the potential to rewrite your story.

You have successfully captured the vision you want to create. You are determined to go the distance and not leave any parts behind. You have everything you need to make your epic vision a reality. You have connected with your highest self and made space to receive the abundance you desire.

Now that you've done all this, what's next for you? You need to amplify and speed up your vision by working with time to deliver your epic vision faster. Align your time with the frequency of making your vision come true.

Remember, reinventing yourself and writing a new chapter in your life is inevitable and essential.

You have realized that the one standing in your way is now out of your way.

You now have access to your superpowers and an abundance ready to manifest your epic vision.

You are a vision-manifester.

Everything you desire flows easily and abundantly.

You're now unstoppable. Go and live your epic life!

Moment of Reflection

Fadhwa Yusuf

Printed in Great Britain
by Amazon

48378051R00118